My Heart *in* His Hands

Summer

Set Me Free Indeed

VONETTE
Zachary
BRIGHT

New*Life*
PUBLICATIONS

My Heart in His Hands:
Set Me Free Indeed

Published by
NewLife Publications
A ministry of Campus Crusade for Christ
P.O. Box 620877
Orlando, FL 32862-0877

Production by Genesis Group

Edited by Brenda Josee, Tammy Campbell, Joette Whims, and Lynn Copeland

Cover by Koechel Peterson Design

Printed in the United States of America

ISBN 1-56399-162-4

For more information, write:

Campus Crusade for Christ International—100 Lake Hart Drive, Orlando, FL 32832, USA

L.I.F.E., Campus Crusade for Christ—P.O. Box 40, Flemington Markets, 2129, Australia

Campus Crusade for Christ of Canada—Box 529, Sumas, WA 98295

Campus Crusade for Christ—Fairgate House, King's Road, Tyseley, Birmingham, B11 2AA, United Kingdom

Lay Institute for Evangelism, Campus Crusade for Christ—P.O. Box 8786, Auckland, 1035, New Zealand

Campus Crusade for Christ—9 Lock Road #3-03, PacCan Centre, Singapore

Great Commission Movement of Nigeria—P.O. Box 500, Jos, Plateau State, Nigeria, West Africa

Contents

A Note of Thanks

love being a woman. My mother made womanhood seem so special. She enjoyed working in the marketplace, but in no way deprived her family. I owe my visions of womanhood to her. My desire as a Christian woman has been not only to present the gospel to all who would listen, but to encourage women to be all they can be. They do this by finding their identity in Jesus Christ and their fulfillment in His plan for their life, then exerting their influence to improve the welfare of their home, community, nation, and the world.

I believe women largely hold the moral key to society. To mobilize them for the cause of Christ, Women Today International was created. Mary Graham, a twenty-seven-year Crusade staff member, co-directed this ministry, helped launch the radio program *Women Today with Vonette Bright*, and served as its producer. The scripts for these daily programs form the basis of this book— daily nuggets to help women find answers and encouragement, cope with circumstances, and realize their significance and influence.

To extend the ministry of the radio program was a dream of Brenda Josee. She is a good friend and a great encouragement to me. Her beautiful and creative ideas have made this book a reality. She and Tammy Campbell compiled, organized, and edited the scripts, and Joette Whims and Lynn Copeland gave the material a final edit. I also thank my dear husband, Bill, my greatest source of inspiration and encouragement, with whom I have enjoyed the adventure of trusting God for over fifty years.

My heartfelt thanks go to:

The current and former staff of *Women Today*—Judy Clark, Sallie Clingman, Pam Davis, Cherry Fields, Tina Hood, Liz Lazarian, JoAnn Lynch Licht, Robin Maroudi, Patty McClung, Kathy MacLeod, Judy Nelson, Anna Patterson, Laura Staudt Sherwood, Pam Sloop, Mary Ann White, Carrie Wright; the script writers—Christy Brain, Lisa Brockman, Rebecca Cotton, Angie Bruckner Grella, Keva Harrison, Kirsten Jarrett, Roger Kemp, Cindy Kinkaid, Tracy Lambert, Christi Mansfield, Linda Wall, Kara Austin Williams, Ann Wright; "The Committee" in Orlando; The Lighthouse Report; Ambassador Advertising; Evelyn Gibson; and Jim Sanders.

All of this to say, this book has been a gift to me from the hard work of others. I now present it to you. My prayer is that these devotionals will be an encouragement to you and will help you in a greater way to entrust *your heart into His hands.*

My dear friends,

The decision is now in the hands of the jury." We understand these familiar words.

"I will take matters into my own hands." Again, we know exactly what that means. Because we take hold of things physically with our hands, our hands symbolize control of situations, emotions, and ideas.

How many times have you asked someone, "Can you handle that?" There is One who is able to perfectly handle every aspect of your life. If you have accepted the Lord Jesus Christ as your Savior, the best way to describe the security of not only this life on earth, but also the eternal destiny of your soul, is to picture *your heart in the hands of God!*

The God who promised the descendants of Abraham, "I will uphold you with my righteous right hand" (Isaiah 41:10) also holds your heart in His hands.

Life is often hectic, and the responsibilities of women in our culture place enormous demands on our physical and emotional energy. By the time we meet the needs of the day, we may find little time to seek God's heart and find solace in the strength of His hands.

I love to see a mother cradle the head of her crying newborn in her hands and gently stroke away the tears.

The security that infant feels with the familiar touch of his mother calms him to sleep. That's the scene I picture when I come to God in prayer for my own needs and express my frustrations to Him. Just sitting quietly before Him, I can sense His gentle touch caressing my aching heart, and my burden is soon lifted.

King David said it so perfectly: "You open your hand and satisfy the desires of every living thing" (Psalm 145:16).

If you have not placed your heart in His hands, please do so today. You may have accepted the Lord Jesus as your Savior but are still struggling in your life because you don't know the security, comfort, and guidance of His hand. The psalmist assures you:

He who dwells in the shelter of the Most High
will rest in the shadow of the Almighty.
I will say of the LORD, "He is my refuge and my fortress,
my God, in whom I trust." (Psalm 91:1,2)

Give Him your whole heart and experience the peace and joy that will follow you through every season of your life.

From my joyful heart to yours,

Vonette Z. Bright

Our Hearts Set Free

If the Son sets you free, you will be free indeed.

JOHN 8:36

Warm weather brings with it many welcome changes. Short days and cold wintry nights are exchanged for open doors and windows and long evenings for picnics and ballgames. The confinement of winter gives way to the freedom of summer.

On a lovely summer day after my freshman year in college, I received a letter from Bill Bright. I remembered Bill from our school days. He was in business in California, and if that wasn't enough to impress a girl, the stationery read, "Bright's California Confections." I responded with a ten-page letter. That letter, that summer day, was the beginning of a beautiful romance.

Perhaps you could capture the joy of the summer

season by renewing an old acquaintance. Encourage your children to write letters or make creative note cards to send to family and friends.

With our hectic lifestyles, it's easy to lose contact with friends or to not know those who live next door. Make an effort to get to know your neighbors and practice "friendship evangelism." Ponder the words of 1 John 1:7: "If we walk in the light, as he is in the light, we have fellowship with one another…"

Let this summer season be a time of walking in the light that shines supernaturally *in* and *on* and *through* you. Determine to pursue the heart of God and allow Him to empower you to express the most precious freedom a woman can know—freedom from the bondage of sin and guilt—given by a merciful God through His Son Jesus Christ.

The Creator of the seasons will hold your heart in His hands, providing safety and security for a life of true joy. The desire for freedom deep within the heart of every human being is part of the great Creator's design. True freedom, which comes only from God, enables you to be wise and compassionate.

The ultimate reality of true freedom is expressed in the choice we have to place our heart in the hands of God. What a privilege!

The Free Heart

The Spirit of the Lord is on me,
because he has anointed me
to preach good news to the poor.
He has sent me to proclaim freedom
for the prisoners
and recovery of sight for the blind,
to release the oppressed,
to proclaim the year of the Lord's favor.

LUKE 4:18,19

The cry for freedom in the '70s encompassed everything from clothing to occupations. Unfortunately, some of the zeal to express freedom lead to acts of rebellion.

True freedom, however, brings responsibility. Paul writes, "You, my [sisters], were called to be free. But do not use your freedom to indulge the sinful nature; rather, serve one another in love" (Galatians 5:13). Knowing Christ, the source of our freedom, we are free to express our individuality, pursue satisfying career goals, and have meaningful relationships. We fulfill the command to "live as free [women], but do not use your freedom as a cover-up for evil; live as servants of God" (1 Peter 2:16).

The desire for freedom within each individual is no surprise to any mother. Children learn to express their desire for freedom at quite a young age. Childish innocence can be dangerous, so the guiding hand of a mother protects a child from harm and injury.

A woman who has accepted Jesus Christ as her Savior has a powerful Protector—the Holy Spirit who indwells her. He will guide her thought life and guard her heart from the evil one. But let us not think only of the ways freedom must be restrained. We need to accept the beautiful freedom we have in Christ and to live a life that demonstrates freedom of originality, creativity, and expression, and encourages others to find ways to enjoy the freedom that comes from knowing Christ.

Guilt, shame, and responsibility. That's what Julian began to feel. But it took him seventeen long years to get there.

In 1977, he committed a horrendous violent crime. He and an accomplice broke into a home in Southern California. Mary Stein, 73, was home at the time.

The two criminals beat her to death with a piece of wood. Remarkably, during the beating, Mary Stein called out to God, "Oh, Lord, I'm coming home."

Clear Conscience

Like a laser imprint, Mary's last words burned into Julian's mind, haunting him. A year after the murder, he placed his trust in Jesus Christ.

Soon, the guilt, the shame, and the sense of responsibility for killing Mary Stein began to set in. God began rebuilding this man's once-corrupted conscience. As Julian grew in his faith, God continued to establish a foundation of morals, values, and conscience.

The police did not actively consider him a suspect. But those feelings of guilt, shame, and responsibility didn't go away. They only intensified.

In God's timing—some seventeen years after the

murder—Julian did what God and his conscience told him to do. He confessed his crime.

Today, he's serving a prison sentence for the murder. But the freedom in his heart cannot be confined.

Friend, that's what knowing God is all about. God paid the price for sin by giving His only Son. When you confess your sin to Him and place your trust in Him, He forgives you. Like Julian, your heart will be free from the bondage of sin.

It's never too late to turn to Christ—to confess your sin, to clear your conscience. You can do that right now. See "Beginning Your Journey of Joy" at the back of this book to learn how.

Remember, God loves you more than you know. He wants to give you life, eternal life.

HIS WORD

"He who conceals his sins does not prosper, but whoever confesses and renounces them finds mercy" *(Proverbs 28:13).*

MY PART

Is there some sin from the past that is pricking your conscience? Whatever it is, confess it to God. He will forgive you, and He will lead you to make things right, however difficult. Then you will know true freedom.

MY STUDY

Joel 2:32; Romans 6:17,18

Becky's grandmother was larger than life to her children and grandchildren. They lovingly called her "Big Mama." She was the grand matriarch of the family.

Loved and adored by all, she was the glue that held the family together. Her unflinching faith in God gave great stability to a family torn by death and divorce.

Be Certain

Her first husband had died unexpectedly, leaving her with four children. She worked hard to keep food on the table. Later, she fell in love and married again. She and her second husband had four more children. Sadly, the marriage ended in divorce. She was left alone, but this time with a total of eight children.

Through it all, her abiding faith in God never wavered.

Big Mama had a big, well-worn Bible next to her favorite chair. It was so obvious she loved God. She depended on Him completely, and He always came through.

Big Mama lived with her eldest son and his wife. Like Big Mama, they trusted God and walked faithfully with Him.

Many years after Big Mama died, Becky visited her aunt. As she was leaving, she said to her aunt a bit offhandedly, "I'll see you here, there, or in the air."

"I hope so," her aunt responded.

Shocked, Becky said, "What do you mean you *hope* so?"

From the ensuing conversation, Becky discovered that neither her aunt nor Big Mama had complete confidence in their eternal destiny.

Becky was so sorry to learn that her grandmother was uncertain about whether she'd go to heaven when she died. She'd never enjoyed the peace and assurance God wanted her to have.

My friend, God says if you place your faith in Him, He gives you eternal life. There's no uncertainty in His promise.

When God makes a promise, He keeps it! He promises you freedom and a place in heaven. Trust Him.

HIS WORD

"To as many as did receive and welcome Him, He gave the authority (power, privilege, right) to become the children of God, that is, to those who believe in (adhere to, trust in, and rely on) His name" (John 1:12, Amplified).

MY PART

Do you have any doubts about where you will go when you die? If you have accepted Christ as your Savior, the Bible says you are a child of God and will spend eternity in heaven. If you still have doubts, search God's Word for His promises or talk to your pastor.

MY STUDY
Psalm 16:9,10; Isaiah 60:3

Kris was ten years old when she asked Jesus to be her Savior. To this day, she remembers that moment as if it were yesterday.

Kris had trusted Christ with her life, but her parents didn't teach the Bible in their home. Her family prayed at mealtimes and went to church on Sundays, but that was about all.

Pour Out Your Heart

Eventually, no one in her family went to church but Kris. Even as a young teenager, Kris would go to church with friends or alone. Kris knew that she'd made a commitment to follow Christ, but she didn't know how to grow or how to ask someone to help her grow.

Doubt about her commitment to Jesus Christ crept into her heart and nagged her for about ten years. During that period of doubt, she asked Jesus to come into her heart every day! But she continued to go to church and Bible studies.

Finally, in her early twenties, Kris told a friend

about her struggle. After a long discussion, the friend said, "Kris, you need to pour out your heart to God."

So Kris spent a long time alone talking with God. She told Him everything on her mind. She remembers only these words: "God, I'm tired of not knowing if You're in my life. If You're real, help me know with certainty." Nothing dramatic happened, but about two weeks later, Kris began to notice a few changes.

First, she hadn't questioned God about His presence in her life or hadn't asked Christ into her life since that day.

Also, when she read the Bible, it was making sense to her like never before. All of her doubt was gone!

Dear friend, maybe you feel like Kris did. Pour out your heart to God. Read His Word. And most importantly, trust Him.

HIS WORD
"Trust in him at all times, O people; pour out your hearts to him, for God is our refuge" (Psalm 62:8).

MY PART
Right now, talk with God. Tell Him everything. Ask Him to help you know He's real and He's in your heart. He's a faithful God. I'm confident He'll do for you what He did for Kris. Ask Him today. Your life will never be the same.

MY STUDY
Isaiah 12:2; 1 John 5:11–15

DAY 4

everal years ago, my friend Ney Bailey was traveling in a country where Christianity is strictly forbidden. For decades, its citizens have been under the thumb of a hostile, controlling government.

While touring the countryside, Ney saw a woman and asked, through an interpreter, if she could take her picture. To Ney's delight, the woman was pleased to have her photo taken by an American tourist. After the camera snapped, she thanked Ney by saying, "Go in peace."

True Liberty

Ney responded, "May the Lord's peace be upon you."

Later, the interpreter told Ney that the woman had been quite bold to say, "Go in peace." It's the greeting of a believer, and for her to reveal herself to a foreigner was quite risky.

Thousands of miles from home, in the middle of nowhere, standing in a cornfield in a country where it was unlawful to be a Christian, Ney met a sister in Christ. Although they could not communicate in each other's language, they recognized the Spirit in the other and made a powerful connection.

Ney captured this moment in a picture that has ministered to many of us. The woman's wrinkled and weatherworn face reveals a very hard life. Even so, her radiance glows. Though she lives in bondage, she is personally free.

In Galatians 5:1 we read, "It is for freedom that Christ has set us free. Stand firm, then, and do not let yourselves be burdened again by a yoke of slavery."

Where we place our faith determines our liberty. If we trust in ourselves, we are bound by our own limitations. If we trust in the government, we are bound by what it can provide. If we trust in any human institution, *we are bound to be disappointed!*

But when we place our faith in God through the person of Jesus Christ, we experience true liberty.

HIS WORD
"If the Son sets you free, you will be free indeed" (John 8:36).

MY PART
"Lord Jesus, thank You for being a loving, faithful God. May I learn to depend more and more on You each day and not on the attractions of this world. You alone are worthy of my trust. In Your holy name, amen."

MY STUDY
Psalm 86:12,13; Isaiah 61:1

ear plagues many in our society today, stopping them dead in their tracks. But fear is nothing new.

The greatest story ever told, the Christmas story, contains several references to fear. Reread the accounts in Matthew 1–2 and Luke 1–2. Four times in the story, God speaks to His people and used the same exact wording: "Do not be afraid."

Do Not Be Afraid

He said it first to Zechariah, the priest who "was gripped with fear." Then He said it to Joseph, the fiancé of Mary. Next, to Mary, the one who would be the mother of our Lord. Finally, He said it to the shepherds on the hillside, "Do not be afraid."

So what did these people do with their fear? They did exactly what God wanted them to do:

- The priest completed his time of service.
- Joseph accepted Mary as his wife even though she was pregnant.
- Mary carried and gave birth to our Lord Jesus.

- The shepherds went to Bethlehem just as they'd been told. That's the model. When you're afraid, do exactly what God has called you to do. As you obey, your fear will be replaced with peace and joy.

You can let worries and concerns frighten and enslave you, or you can choose, like those men and women in the Christmas story, to do what God wants you to do. Dear friend, what does He want you to do? *Trust Him!* Begin right there. Surrender your life to the lordship of Christ. Ask Him to fill you with His Holy Spirit. By faith, claim the strength you need to obey His Word.

Experience the freedom from fear that God wants you to have. God has not left us without a Resource. The Holy Spirit will help you overcome fear as you place your circumstances in His hands.

HIS WORD
"Seek first his kingdom and his righteousness, and all these things will be given to you as well. Therefore do not worry about tomorrow, for tomorrow will worry about itself. Each day has enough trouble of its own" (Matthew 6:33,34).

MY PART
What are you afraid of today? What anxious thoughts consume you? There's no need to be afraid. You can surrender all your anxieties to God —this very moment. He can handle anything. Trust Him and you'll have peace.

MY STUDY
Jeremiah 7:23; Psalm 23:4

DAY 6

For most children, every day is filled with carefree adventure. But tragically for some, life is bound with pain, fear, and disappointment.

That's the way it was for Adam.

Mary first heard about him in her prayer group. It was there that Adam's schoolteacher prayed for him. His family life was so fractured and he was so distraught that he saw no future, no escape. At the tender age of eight years old, Adam told his teacher he wanted to die.

Despair No More

Deeply moved and concerned for this little boy, Mary began to pray in earnest for Adam, a little boy she didn't even know.

The next week, Mary was at church, rushing to get to choir rehearsal on time. As she rounded a corner, she and a little boy almost collided. He was also in a hurry and was quite upset. Mary noticed his tears and asked him his name. "Adam," he said.

Suddenly, Mary sensed this was the little boy she'd been praying for all week long. She said, "Where are you going, Adam?"

He admitted, "I'm running away because I want to die."

At that very moment, Adam was heading out of church to get some drugs he had stashed. He was on the way to ending his life.

Mary sat with Adam and held him, sharing the love of God with this distraught little boy. She told him that he was Jesus' little boy and could tell Him all of his secrets. Adam cried and cried.

As Mary prayed for little Adam, God's love penetrated his broken heart. And when the prayer was finished, Adam looked back at Mary with a new light in his eyes.

A chance meeting. A few moments of love. A hug. A welcome prayer. And a life is changed—from one of despair and disappointment into one of hope.

HIS WORD
"There is surely a future hope for you, and your hope will not be cut off" (Proverbs 23:18).

MY PART
Dear friend, many around you do not have the hope that you and I do. Always be prepared to share with them the reason for your hope, to share what Christ has done in your life. Then pray for God to make you sensitive to opportunities to do so.

MY STUDY
Isaiah 40:30,31; Romans 15:13

Maria was only forty-five years old. It appeared that there was nothing the doctors could do. She had only two days to live and needed to get her house in order.

Maria went home and started doing the laundry. She was getting her house in order—right? But she soon realized that getting her house in order was about relationships, not laundry. Immediately, she thought about her stepfather.

Putting Your House in Order

This man had abused her as a child. She despised him and hated her mother for allowing the abuse to happen.

A few years earlier when her mother became very ill, she desperately needed care, and wanted to come live with Maria. In spite of her misgivings, Maria agreed.

Her mother, normally very reserved, reached out and took hold of Maria's hand. In that moment, Maria was convicted of her hatred for her mother. Christ melted her heart. They forgave each other, and her mother received Christ. Three days later Maria's mother slipped into a coma and died.

Now Maria was close to death herself. Maria had never released the bitterness she felt toward her stepfather and knew that it was time to let go of it and let God heal her heart. In prayer, she gave over to God all the hatred she harbored.

Through a series of miracles, one of which involved the surgical skill of a wonderful cardiologist, Maria made it through her life-threatening situation and is alive today to tell this account of God's healing. More important, she was able to be at her stepfather's side when he died, sharing the gospel with him in the final moments of his life.

Friend, don't allow your life to be destroyed by bitterness and hatred. Give it to God. He is able to heal your broken heart, and only He is able to put your house in order.

HIS WORD

"If your enemy is hungry, give him food to eat; if he is thirsty, give him water to drink" (Proverbs 25:21).

MY PART

At times, we all have events in our lives that might cause us to become bitter. These events can enslave us, but God wants us to have freedom. That means we must forgive those who have hurt us. Is there someone you need to forgive? Do it today.

MY STUDY

1 Samuel 24:8–13; Luke 6:27–36

Lori's life was turned upside-down when she was a junior in college. A young man she thought was a friend needed a ride home. She obliged. He led her into his apartment and raped her four times throughout the night, then let her go in the morning.

When her boyfriend found out what happened, he left her. For months, the rapist taunted and degraded her. Even though Lori was a Christian and grew up in the church, she began to believe his lies. Many times she came close to taking her own life.

Overcome the Aftershocks

Nothing in Lori's upbringing prepared her for this. She was in a state of shock and was gripped by fear. Nighttime was unbearable. Every noise terrified her. She was desperately seeking anything that would bring security.

Finally, Lori shared her dilemma with two godly older women. They graciously led her to the Word of God and showed her how to combat her fear.

The more Lori read her Bible, the more help she found. She said, "In three days, I had no more fear and haven't had any fear since."

Lori's story is a graphic reminder of how important the Word of God is in our lives. It's not only important to read it, it's vital to memorize it. The beauty and wisdom of God's words give us quick access to His power and comfort.

I realize that I'm speaking to two kinds of people: those who are, at this moment, trying to recover from a personal disaster and those who will experience one in the future. Both of you can overcome the aftershocks of fear.

I encourage you to seek comfort in the Lord and gain strength from His Word. Commit meaningful verses to memory and rely on these verses to guide your life. You won't be disappointed! God's Word will never fail you.

HIS WORD
"When you pass through the waters, I will be with you; and when you pass through the rivers, they will not sweep over you. When you walk through the fire, you will not be burned; the flames will not set you ablaze" (Isaiah 43:2).

MY PART
Memorizing God's Word is a valuable tool for combating the temptations that attack us everyday. Try this, my friend. Purpose in your heart to memorize one verse a week for at least the next month —perhaps the verses provided in this book. You'll be glad you did.

MY STUDY
Psalm 4:1; John 14:27

For some, being diagnosed with cancer is a death sentence. For Edwina Perkins it meant a new lease on life.

A 31-year-old mother of two, Edwina never dreamed the lump she found in her breast could be cancer. Confident the biopsy would reveal nothing, Edwina made the 45-minute drive to her doctor alone.

A New Lease on Life

Normally quite jovial, the doctor was somber. He faced Edwina and said those words every woman fears: "I'm sorry. It's cancer."

On the long drive home, Edwina was not alone. God was there. Edwina reviewed a mental checklist of things that were important to her and things that were not. She decided right then that it was time to get rid of her number one problem—anger.

All her life, Edwina had been an angry person, harboring hurt and resentment, letting anger simmer and stew. As a Christian, she knew this was wrong, but nothing seemed to help. She'd memorized the verses in

Ephesians 4:26,27, which say: "Do not let the sun go down while you are still angry, and do not give the devil a foothold." She desperately wanted to let go of anger. She just didn't know how.

Now, returning home to share the bad news with her family, Edwina made a vow. "I will no longer allow anger to rule my life," she prayed. "I want it to be gone!"

Through surgery, chemotherapy, and radiation treatments, Edwina survived the fight with breast cancer. To this day, anger no longer characterizes her life.

Oh sure, she gets upset, but she doesn't allow herself to burn with those old feelings. She chooses to let things go so that anger won't rob her of one more day's joy.

That's what God wants for you. Friend, don't wait for a scrape with death to begin living the abundant life. Start living God's best right now!

HIS WORD
"Refrain from anger and turn from wrath; do not fret—it leads only to evil" (Psalm 37:8).

MY PART
"Loving heavenly Father, please forgive me for those times when I hold on to my anger. Anger steals my joy. Help me to always be patient and quick to forgive—as You are patient and forgiving of me. In Jesus' holy name, amen."

MY STUDY
Ecclesiastes 7:9
James 1:19,20

Corrie ten Boom, my personal mentor, spent many years in a concentration camp during World War II. While there, she was constantly degraded, but never more so than in the delousing shower.

Corrie felt she had—by grace—forgiven those cruel men who had robbed her of her dignity while guarding the shower stalls.

Paid in Full

Years later, Corrie was speaking on forgiveness in a church in Munich. After the sermon, a man came toward her with his hand outstretched. Corrie's heart froze. Here was one of the very men who had stood outside the camp shower and leered at her and the others.

She thought, "I cannot forgive. I cannot forgive. Oh, God, forgive me. I cannot forgive." As Corrie gave her resentment to the Lord, she felt the forgiveness of God for *her* lack of forgiveness. Corrie's heart melted and she extended her hand to him.

A debt was owed to her, but she chose to release it. The sword of God's truth surgically removed this blemish on Corrie's heart.

Friend, just like Corrie, you too can release a debt

owed to you and be set free.

First, acknowledge that you've been hurt. Be very specific about the injustice. Write it down.

Second, determine what that person owes you. What do you want from here? This is where a lot of people create false expectations, and it really helps to define what you want. Write that down.

Third, honestly consider the likelihood that you'll never get paid, that you'll never get what you want.

Then, finish by writing these words at the bottom: "Paid in full. Debt retired."

Let the debt go. Say, "I'm not going to require justice here. The debt that is owed me is gone. I've forgiven that, and I'm not going to take that debt back."

That's heart surgery! The process may hurt and take time, but it's definitely worth the effort. You will be free indeed.

HIS WORD

"Do not say, 'I'll do to him as he has done to me; I'll pay that man back for what he did'" (Proverbs 24:29).

MY PART

"Lord Jesus, I owed a great debt. You came to earth, were beaten, bruised, and crucified; and on the third day, You arose. All this to pay for my debt. I am humbled beyond measure by this gracious gift. Help me to forgive those who owe me a debt. Thank You, my Savior, amen."

MY STUDY

Exodus 23:4–6
Colossians 3:13

Cristi was dissatisfied with her singleness. Growing up, her family and church promoted the idea that she was made for a man. It seemed that marriage was the only road to happiness.

Her desire was to serve the Lord by being the best wife and mother possible. But Cristi's hopes were shattered after two serious relationships ended in disappointment.

Satisfaction

Finally, she realized that for years most of her prayers had been about her desires for marriage. She had been seeking relationships rather than the Giver of relationships. Only God could love her unconditionally. Relationships come and go, but His love and fellowship remain constant.

So she completely gave her life over to God by praying, "Lord, if marriage isn't in Your plans for me, then I don't want to waste my life in the waiting room. Please show me what You would have me do."

The process of surrendering her desires was not easy. But as she concentrated on getting to know the Lord better and sought His purpose for her life, God began to work in her.

She left her career as a newspaper journalist and began writing for a Christian magazine where her newfound desire for ministry could be fulfilled.

Cristi developed intimate, lifelong friendships with her roommates. She invited her friends' children over for slumber parties. She met weekly with a high school sophomore for Bible study. She even planned activities for singles at her church.

My friend, if you ever struggle with dissatisfaction—whether single or married—rethink your situation. No man can ever perfectly fulfill your needs or help you live your life to the fullest. Only God can do that.

Pursue His unique purpose for your life and place your desires in His hands. Only then can you reach the potential He has in mind for you.

HIS WORD

"I will betroth you to me forever; I will betroth you in righteousness and justice, in love and compassion" (Hosea 2:19).

MY PART

Friend, are you ever dissatisfied with your life? First, consider the source of your dissatisfaction. Is it God or man? If it's man, you are not pursuing God wholeheartedly. If it's God, He is trying to move you in a different direction. Whichever it is, listen to God's leading.

MY STUDY

1 Timothy 6:6;
Proverbs 15:16

remember vividly the day Bill and I helped our youngest son, Brad, pack his car to move to Washington, D.C. He was leaving home to launch his new career.

As we walked him out to the car, my mind wandered back to the many other times we'd said good-bye to Brad. Each time, I had to realize that my two sons have never belonged to us in the first place. They were entrusted to us by God, and the goal all along had been their independence. Now both our sons have children of their own and our nest is empty.

The Empty Nest

The good news is that the empty-nest syndrome doesn't have to be deadly. It can be the beginning of a richer, fuller life. Many couples find profound satisfaction during this period.

If you find yourself with an empty nest or if you're getting ready for this stage, let me offer four suggestions.

First, *let go*. As our children become mature adults, we must consciously give them back to God's care.

Second, *accept the change*. Nothing you do will bring them back. Instead, take advantage of a great opportunity. Both you and your husband have changed over the years. Enjoy the adventure of a greater intimacy and a creative partnership with each other.

Third, *adopt a positive attitude.* Self-pity and inflexibility only make a difficult transition harder. But a positive outlook opens our hearts and minds to the Lord's healing and helps to ease the pain.

Fourth, *walk into the future.* Use the empty nest as a stepping-stone toward living a purposeful life. Prayerfully decide with your husband which direction the Lord wants you to take, and use your extra time, energy, and money to make a difference.

Friend, there doesn't need to be emptiness in your home when God is there. It can be full of the joy and abundance only He can bring!

HIS WORD
"Serve the LORD with fear and rejoice with trembling" (Psalm 2:11).

MY PART
"Oh Father, let me be sensitive to the leading of Your Spirit in making choices that will honor You and contribute most to our marriage and lifetime goals. I place my heart in Your hands. Amen."

MY STUDY
Colossians 3:23,24
Isaiah 43:2

In his book A *View from the Zoo*, Gary Richmond, pastor and former zookeeper, described the day he received a telephone call from the head veterinarian. They needed to perform surgery on the eyelids of a king cobra.

Let It Go

This was a physically demanding procedure that required several men. It involved capturing the snake and holding it down on the table. For twenty-minutes, the doctor would perform the tedious surgery.

A team gathered in the operating room and, together, managed to bring the snake down. When uncoiled, the cobra was over six feet long.

Once they grabbed the snake, Gary was assigned to hold the snake by the back of the neck for the duration of the surgery. For the entire procedure, the fangs of the cobra discharged yellow venom—enough poison to kill hundreds of men.

When the surgery was finally completed, the doctor looked at Gary and said, "You need to know that the easy part is grabbing hold of the snake. The hard part is letting go."

Sin is like that cobra, isn't it? It's often much easier to grab hold of something very dangerous than it is to let it go.

In life there are many temptations. Something may appear harmless on the outside, but once you have it in your grip, it becomes a habit. Before long, you can't let go.

My friend, be sure you're not allowing anything to enter your life that you won't be able to let go—whether it's what you're reading or watching, something you're drinking or eating, or the friends with whom you are associating.

There's nothing the enemy would like more than finding something that will capture your attention and take your focus off the Lord. Give those issues to the Lord, and trust Him to give you the strength to resist. He wants to help you. And He will!

HIS WORD
"You, dear children, are from God and have overcome them, because the one who is in you is greater than the one who is in the world" (1 John 4:4).

MY PART
Do you have anything in your life that has the potential to take your sights off the Lord—something no one knows about or that seems insignificant? Friend, be careful. Refocus your life on Christ. Take time in prayer now to turn the temptation over to Him and begin to rely on Him alone.

MY STUDY
Genesis 3:1–19; Proverbs 1:10–16

The late Dr. Louis Evans, a dear friend, told this story from his childhood experience.

As a young boy, he and some of his playmates found a dead bird. They decided it needed a decent burial, so they made a shoebox casket and dug a hole. Then they chose one of the friends to preach at the bird's funeral and another to sing. Ceremoniously, they dropped the makeshift casket into the earth.

Just Bury It

They had so much fun that the next day they decided to dig up the box and have another funeral! This time someone else preached and someone else sang.

The next day they did it again with different roles for different friends.

Finally, Louis's father realized what they were doing and put a stop to it. He said, "Boys, leave that bird buried! When something is dead, you don't keep digging it up again!"

A simple, innocent story, but the lesson is profound, isn't it?

The Bible says, "If we confess our sins, he is faithful and just and will forgive us our sins and purify us from all unrighteousness" (1 John 1:9). When John wrote these words, he knew that even Christians continue to sin. But when you become aware of your sin, you need to confess it. You simply agree with God that you were wrong.

Then, you can *know* you're forgiven. Even your guilt and shame are removed. God never brings it up again.

Yet too many times forgiven Christians are tempted to dig up old stuff, to revisit issues that have already been resolved. They don't know that they've been forgiven.

When you don't know you're forgiven, the guilt will rob you of peace with God and prevent you from reaching out to others with the true message of God's love and forgiveness.

My friend, your sins are buried and forgotten—don't keep digging them up!

HIS WORD
"As far as the east is from the west, so far has he removed our transgression from us" (Psalm 103:12).

MY PART
I encourage you to read the book of 1 John. When you do, pay attention to the number of times the word "know" is used in that book. This will help you to stop digging up the things that God wants to leave buried. Your sins are forever forgiven!

MY STUDY
Isaiah 43:25
Hebrews 10:22

Fifteen years ago when Peggy was pregnant, her husband insisted she have an abortion, and tragically, she obliged. The guilt and remorse that followed were far beyond Peggy's anticipation. She fell into deep depression, and her marriage fell apart.

The Healing Touch

When Peggy became a Christian, God began to work in her heart. She was employed as a computer operator during the week and served as the singles' director for her church on the weekends.

Peggy kept her secret locked up tight. She was afraid of rejection if she told the truth.

Eventually, she decided to let her friends and associates know about her past. She wanted to be honest and to help others avoid the same mistake.

Peggy saw God take the most horrible event in her life—the death of her baby—and replace it with an abundance of love for others. Today, Peggy invests her time reaching young children in the inner city. Through creative outreach programs, Peggy finds joy in bringing the good news to underprivileged families.

When Peggy trusted God, He forgave her. He also gave her a new purpose in life.

Maybe you're struggling with a hard issue like Peggy's. It may not be abortion, but perhaps something else is hindering you in your relationship with God.

Be encouraged, my friend. Seek His forgiveness, and see what He will do.

The tragedy of Peggy's past became the springboard for her present ministry. She's able to reach out to others. They respond to her heart of compassion because they know she understands. She's been right where they are.

Don't let the tragedy of your past mistakes keep you from experiencing the fullness He wants to give you in the present.

Open your heart to the Lord today. Let Him reach into your life with His healing touch. Then you will have what it takes to reach out to others.

HIS WORD

"Praise be to the God and Father of our Lord Jesus Christ, the Father of compassion and the God of all comfort, who comforts us in all our troubles, so that we can comfort those in any trouble with the comfort we ourselves have received from God" (2 Corinthians 1:3,4).

MY PART

"God of all comfort, you know the pain in my heart. Please reach into my life today and heal the wounds of yesterday that keep me from living to the fullest. Show me how to use my past experiences to help others. Amen."

MY STUDY

Genesis 50:20; Psalm 40:1–3

A family was staying in a high-rise condo on the beach. As the mother walked into the living room, terror filled her heart. Her three-year-old son was perched precariously on the outside of the balcony's guardrail. Hands stretched behind him, he was hanging onto the railing looking down at the beach.

Never Let You Go

She was afraid if she startled him, he'd let go. So despite her panic, she remained calm.

She said softly to her son, "Honey, hold on for Mommy." Then she eased her way up to him. When she was close enough, she thrust out her hands and grabbed his arm—gripping him tightly with the loving force of a caring mother. She breathed a sigh of relief.

The little boy was now secure because one who loved him more than words could ever say had a *never-let-go* grip on him.

My friend, that's a graphic reminder of God's promise that He will never leave you, He'll never let you go.

Consider the determination with which that loving mother held onto that adventurous son. That little guy had no idea how much danger he was in and from what he was being protected!

When you feel like you're dancing on the edge of life, don't worry. The One who loves you more than words can say knew you might feel that way sometimes. So He made it a point to say to you, "Never will I leave you; never will I forsake you" (Hebrews 13:5). He will keep a *never-let-go* grip on you.

There is great freedom in knowing God will never leave you. You can face anything! God is aware of everything in your life and He is with you.

Remember the old song, "He's got the whole world in His hands." Today, picture yourself resting securely in His hands, even if you're on the edge. He will never let you go.

HIS WORD
"The LORD himself goes before you and will be with you; he will never leave you nor forsake you. Do not be afraid; do not be discouraged" (Deuteronomy 31:8).

MY PART
"Ever-present Father, thank You that no matter where I go or what happens to me, You are there—leading, guiding, and protecting. Your comforting, yet firm grip on me is a constant source of security. May I always remember Your strength. In Jesus' mighty name, amen."

MY STUDY
Psalm 9:10; Hebrews 10:23

Some of the most important peo-
ple in my life are single women. The woman who led me
to faith in Christ many years ago was a woman who
never married. She spent her entire life serving the
Lord.

Several of my dearest friends are single. I love them
deeply, and I respect and admire them. They're among
the most dynamic people I know. They're single, and
content.

Single and Content

The Bible contains many examples of women who
weren't married. As far as we know, Mary and Martha
were single adults, and dear friends of Jesus. They are
models of women who opened their home, practiced
hospitality, and reached out to care for the needs of others, including our dear Lord.

Sometimes I look at women I know who've never
married and I wonder why. I so love being married it
makes me want to find husbands for them!

But when I look at their lives and observe how God

is using them, I'm impressed. When I consider the time and energy they're able to devote to the cause of Christ and to others, I'm grateful God has left them single, at least for now.

If you're single, God has a very special plan for you. God wants to use these years in your life in a most unique way.

Today, put your life in God's hands. Then watch how He opens doors. He's promised to meet *your* every need. Whether it's a practical need, an emotional need, or a financial one, He'll take care of you.

If you're lonely, tell Him. If you're afraid, tell Him. If you're confused, tell Him. As you depend on Him, your relationship with Him will grow. And *that* relationship is the only thing on this earth that can meet you at the point of your greatest need and deepest longing.

HIS WORD
"Delight yourself in the LORD and he will give you the desires of your heart" (Psalm 37:4).

MY PART
Are you ever sad that you are not married? Don't despair, my friend. Instead pray, "Lord, I want to trust you with all my life, including my marital status. Please show me how to use my time for Your glory. I'm completely Yours. Amen."

MY STUDY
Isaiah 26:4; Philippians 4:19

Jackie was a student when she came to Christ. She had no understanding of Christianity, but she learned quickly and taught others.

From all appearances, she was solid in her faith and sure of what she believed, but deep in her heart that was not the case. She had put herself on a standard of performance that no one could achieve. She was torturing herself with thoughts of what she should be. *I ought to be better. I ought to do more. I'm not good enough. I'm a failure.*

A Possible Standard

With those destructive thought patterns, Jackie drove herself to succeed. When she was successful, she felt proud. When she failed, she condemned herself and felt as though God condemned her, too. As this negative spiral went on for years, she was quietly destroying herself.

Finally, she fell apart emotionally and cried out for help. She knew this couldn't be the Christian life—trying to be perfect and hating herself for failing.

She studied God's grace. She read, talked with her

friends, and prayed. Eventually, she understood.

Today, Jackie is like a new person. Understanding the grace of God transformed her life. She is a marriage and family therapist who specializes in family abuse issues.

If God were the hard taskmaster Jackie feared, none of us could bear it. In our humanity, we could never live up to His perfect standard. So we have only two options: give up or hide. Jackie was one of the many who hid. She couldn't let anyone see her weakness. She had to pretend it wasn't there.

Once she realized that God is a God of grace, everything changed. God knows we're not perfect. We only need to receive His acceptance, forgiveness, and grace. He doesn't ask us to change ourselves or perform to some impossible standard, but just to trust Him and let Him change our lives.

HIS WORD

"Come to me, all you who are weary and burdened, and I will give you rest" (Matthew 11:28).

MY PART

Can you relate to Jackie? Are you trying so hard to fix yourself, doing what you think you should, that you're about to explode? Remember God's grace today. Be honest with Him about where you are and what you need. Then rest. Let His grace transform your life.

MY STUDY

Exodus 33:14; Psalm 68:19

Karen placed her trust in Christ when she was a small child. But when she was eleven years old, her world dramatically changed. A relative abused her, a younger brother died, and her family made a major move. Confusion and pain became a part of her once-peaceful life.

Believe the Truth

She was popular in high school, but that wasn't enough. Looking for more approval and acceptance, she asked a guy friend if she needed to lose weight. "Just a few pounds would help," he answered. Her downward spiral into anorexia had begun.

She immediately set about losing five pounds. It didn't take her long. "It made me feel good," she said. She became even more popular.

She said, "I began to equate love with thinness. I became obsessed with perfection." Whenever Karen consumed calories, she exercised them off.

Her condition worsened. She eventually dropped from 155 pounds to just 82 pounds. She struggled for nine years, coming close to death twice.

One Sunday morning, she was alone in the hospital. She said, "I was face to face with myself." She began to write out a list of lies she'd come to believe. Then she contrasted them with the truth of God and His love, which she'd known deep in her heart for a long time.

She said, "I gave complete control of my life back to God. I asked forgiveness for my self-centeredness, and asked God to help me trust Him to handle my weight."

God answered her prayer. Through extensive therapy, medical help, and the prayers and love of her family and friends, she broke free of the vicious cycle. She gained a more balanced view of herself and a life-changing trust in God.

Friend, I don't know what your day-to-day struggles are. Today, choose to believe the truth of what God says about you. He loves you very deeply just as you are. Remember that always.

HIS WORD
"Then you will know the truth, and the truth will set you free" (John 8:32).

MY PART
"Wonderful Savior, sometimes I forget that it doesn't matter to You how much I weigh or how I look. You love me because I am Your creation. I am precious to You. Help me to see myself through the eyes of truth—Your truth. Amen."

MY STUDY
Psalm 103:6; Hosea 14:9

Dark and dirty and housing almost seven thousand inmates, the 300-year-old Russian prison was a picture of despair.

Ward Coleman and a team of Americans were visiting the prison as part of Operation Carelift, an annual ministry outreach to the people of the former Soviet Union sponsored by the Josh McDowell Ministry.

Peace for Despair

As Ward approached cell number sixteen, a very small metal flap was unlocked by a guard. Immediately, a face appeared. "The face I saw stunned me," Ward said. Unexpectedly, it was the face of a calm and peaceful man—Victor.

Four years earlier, Victor was arrested, charged with a crime and imprisoned, but never convicted. Yet, he was a man at peace.

For a moment, Victor went to the back of his cell. When he returned to the small window, he handed Ward an amazingly intricate sculpture of Christ on the cross. He said, "Give this crucifix to Mr. McDowell. I've read his books. They've helped me so immensely in prison."

Victor explained he'd saved the morsels of bread served with his meals. From those, he molded an ornate cross and a figure of Jesus Christ. For color he used coffee and the vegetables on his plate.

Victor told Ward, "I'm happier now than I've ever been in my life. Before, I had a large apartment, money, and I knew influential people. But now, I have Jesus Christ."

In that moment, Ward thought, *Victor, I'd like to be there where you are, because I sense there's more freedom in there than out here.*

Victor experienced spiritual freedom through God and His Word. No matter what your circumstances, He promises to do the same for you. Today, you may feel trapped in a pit of despair or a sea of pain. You may be a prisoner of debt or addiction. No matter what it is, God knows. He's waiting to help.

HIS WORD
"We are hard pressed on every side, but not crushed; perplexed, but not in despair" (2 Corinthians 4:8).

MY PART
Turn to the Book of Psalms. Dear friend, there's comfort there for whatever you're facing. As you read, listen to God's words of compassion and understanding. Meditate on His truth. It's food for your soul; it's the Bread of Life. And He will set you free.

MY STUDY
Numbers 6:24–26; Psalm 34:14

One day, two children got into big trouble! The older child, Kelly, was given scissors to cut flowers for the table. Her little brother went along to watch.

When the mother checked on the children, she found her son with the scissors and the daughter nowhere in sight. She was angry with Kelly and scared of what could've happened to the young boy with a pair of sharp scissors. When Kelly showed up, she made matters even worse by lying to her mother.

What Sin?

Later that night, after appropriate discipline and apologies, peace was restored to the household. Kelly asked her mother for forgiveness, and it was granted.

The next day, Kelly came to her mother and said, "I feel really bad, Mommy. I feel bad because I lied to you."

"What do you mean?" her mother said.

"Yesterday. When I lied to you. I feel bad."

"Honey, what lie? I've forgotten about that. I forgave you, remember? It's something in the past now."

What a graphic illustration for a little girl who's just learning about forgiveness.

When you and I sin, the Bible instructs us to confess our sin. "Confess" means to agree with God that what we did was wrong. Then we ask for forgiveness. Not only does He forgive completely, He forgets it ever happened.

Corrie ten Boom used to say, "He puts our sin in the deepest ocean and then puts up a 'No Fishing' sign." I love that word picture.

Our human tendency is to remember when we've been wronged. God isn't like that. He forgets and doesn't bring it up again.

Many Christians carry guilt and shame in their hearts, making them feel defeated. Dear friend, it doesn't have to be that way. You are forgiven. When you understand that, you'll want desperately to share that good news with others. Understanding God's love and forgiveness in Christ is the greatest need of our time.

HIS WORD
"I will forgive their wickedness and will remember their sins no more" (Jeremiah 31:34).

MY PART
Ask God to show you anything in your life that's not pleasing to Him. Write it on a sheet of paper. Now ask God to forgive you. Next, write the words of 1 John 1:9 across the page. Thank God for His forgiveness, then tear up the list. The next time you feel guilty about anything on that list, say, "Thank you, Lord. That's forgiven and forgotten. I don't have to worry."

MY STUDY
Psalm 32:1; Ephesians 1:7,8

DAY 22

A correspondent from The Voice of the Martyrs tells how religious cultures clashed in a Muslim country through a simple friendship.

Saleema, 17, was a Christian. Her schoolmate, Raheela, 18, was Muslim. They were friends at school. Saleema often invited Raheela to her home after school.

The Voice of the Martyrs

They talked about God, the God of the Bible. Saleema gave Raheela a Bible and taught her Christian songs. Then Raheela, without her parents' knowledge, would teach the songs to her younger sister.

When Raheela's parents learned about the Christian songs, the younger sister told them where Raheela was learning them.

Saleema invited Raheela to a church service. Raheela heard the gospel and placed her trust in Jesus that day. She grew in her faith, and God changed her life.

Raheela was very open about reading her Bible and praising God. When her family learned of her conversion to Christianity, they were furious. After she refused to accept marriage to a Muslim man, their anger grew, and she ran away.

Raheela's family accused the pastor, his family, and Saleema of kidnapping her. They were arrested, severely beaten, and tortured.

Tragically, Raheela was killed by her own family. Saleema and the pastor were charged with her murder. Through the help of a good lawyer, the charges were eventually reduced to "converting a Muslim."

Our only consolation is *knowing* Raheela is now truly free to worship the Lord Jesus Christ.

The Voice of the Martyrs boldly works to bring us the good news of Jesus Christ's work in countries where Christians are persecuted.

When one member of the Body of Christ suffers, we all suffer. It's my hope that we'll always pray for these dear brothers and sisters who cannot worship as they please.

HIS WORD
"Remember those in prison as if you were their fellow prisoners, and those who are mistreated as if you yourselves were suffering" (Hebrews 13:3).

MY PART
Post Hebrews 13:3 on your refrigerator along with a small map of the world. Use these to remind you to pray for Christians in countries where people are not free to worship the true God. Also pray for continued religious freedom in America and look for ways to share our biblical heritage.

MY STUDY
*Psalm 69;
Isaiah 58:7*

Cindy was a calm and peaceful person. The story of her life, though, is anything but peaceful. She and her second husband lived in several countries, but ended up back in the States after he was diagnosed with a rare form of liver cancer. Before he died, they were fugitives from the law as well as from God.

Do the Right Thing

He was involved in illegal businesses before he met Cindy. After meeting her, he used her good name and credit rating to begin yet another. She didn't know what he was doing, but she knew something wasn't right. The only thing that kept her with him was their young daughter whom he continually threatened to kidnap. So she stayed with him as they ran from justice.

During that time, God caught up with her. She prayed for a way out. When her husband became ill, she made up her mind to surrender. She knew she couldn't keep running, nor did she want to. She wanted to be with her daughter, not go to prison for years. She counted the cost. She knew by turning herself in she might have to face a prison term. But her love for her daughter and her deep desire to do the right thing compelled her.

So Cindy surrendered to authorities. After four days, the judge agreed to set bail for her. Many other miracles followed, and she's now confident that God is working His plan for her life and the life of her daughter.

She's still not completely free, but she's experienced freedom in Christ. Cindy sacrificed to do the right thing.

What is God asking of you? Be obedient to Him today. Sometimes obedience is hard. But God always enables us to make the right choice and follow through. He's promised to provide everything you need and more. Trust Him. He'll make a way.

HIS WORD

"But the man who looks intently into the perfect law that gives freedom, and continues to do this, not forgetting what he has heard, but doing it—he will be blessed in what he does" (James 1:25).

MY PART

Is God asking you to do something that you find difficult? What is keeping you from obedience, my friend? Fear? Pride? God can take care of those things if you will trust Him. Try it. You will be amazed at the results.

MY STUDY

1 Samuel 15:22; Psalm 51:16,17

God wants us to be authentic, not fake. Even the world longs to see people who are real, honest, and consistent.

Being authentic means that we live out in practice what we profess to believe in principle. It means that we say what we mean and mean what we say. It means that we aren't afraid to be vulnerable by expressing the truth, even if we have made a mistake or wronged someone.

Authenticity

We often struggle with being authentic because we're afraid. We think people will perceive us as weak. No one wants to admit she's wrong or doesn't have all the answers. We think this shows weakness when it actually shows strength of character—God's character in you. In the Bible, Christ tells us, "My grace is sufficient for you, for my power is made perfect in weakness" (2 Corinthians 12:9). When we are vulnerable, God's strength is allowed to show in all its glory.

From experience, I can tell you that a person who admits her mistakes is much easier to trust than one who never admits wrong. It is also a command from God. James 5:16 says, "Confess your sins to each other and pray for each other so that you may be healed." Think of it this way. Confession rids the wound of the emotional and spiritual bacteria. Prayer is the agent through which the Holy Spirit heals the wound.

So when you are wrong, be quick to admit it. Don't let it fester into a wound that is difficult or impossible to heal. Instead, express your sorrow and repentance to those you've hurt. This will cleanse your soul of what's ailing it. Your humility is evidence of authenticity—and it honors God.

HIS WORD
"The LORD detests lying lips, but he delights in men who are truthful" (Proverbs 12:22).

MY PART
"God of truth, help me live what I profess. Don't let me proclaim one thing and live another. May people see You in me, in all of my activities. May Your Spirit have such control of me that people will be drawn to You and the life that only You can give. Amen."

MY STUDY
Numbers 5:6,7; James 5:16

Carol was a self-proclaimed worrier. Even her ten-year-old daughter said her mother worried too much. That's when Carol found new perspective from a Bible story popularized in the movie *The Prince of Egypt*, which is about the life of Moses.

God Is in Control

Jochebed, an Israelite and the mother of Moses, had plenty to worry about. When Pharaoh ordered all newborn Israelite boys killed, Jochebed hid her infant son for three months. She knew that she could not hide him forever if he was to have any kind of meaningful life. So she developed a plan and took a chance. Jochebed placed her son in a waterproof basket and sent him down the Nile River. He was rescued by Pharaoh's daughter.

In a miraculous turn, Jochebed was selected as the nurse for the child in Pharaoh's household. Eventually, the loving mother gave Moses to Pharaoh's daughter to be her son.

Jochebed did all she could for her son, then released

him. She probably prayed all the while.

Carol learned how to deal with her worries from this ancient mother. Can you identify with Jochebed or Carol? We all go through times when worry seems to enslave us. But you can have victory over this anxiety. All you have to do is trust God—trust Him because He is all-knowing and all-powerful, and because He loves you. In Romans 8:28, we read, "In all things God works for the good of those who love him, who have been called according to his purpose." He promises to work for our good.

The next time you are worried, remember that God is in control and that He is looking out for you. Then make a conscious effort to stop worrying about things you can't control and start trusting the God who controls all things. You'll live a more peaceful life.

HIS WORD
"Cast all your anxiety on him because he cares for you"
(1 Peter 5:7).

MY PART
The next time you find yourself overwhelmed with worry, try this. Make a list of your worries. Next, develop a plan to take action. Before you begin to work on the steps of your plan, surrender it all to God. We can't control the outcome, but we can take control of our emotions.

MY STUDY
Psalm 37:5–11; Matthew 6:25–34

Do you ever struggle with submitting your desires to God? Maybe you feel that you are giving up your freedom. Or perhaps you think that God will make you do something you won't like.

Surrender

Truthfully, that's the age-old struggle of the Christian life. We often do the very thing we hate. The apostle Paul speaks of this in Romans 7:15: "I do not understand what I do. For what I want to do I do not do, but what I hate I do." As Christians, we know right from wrong, but as humans, we still have fleshly desires pulling at us. Tragically, sometimes they win.

This can be especially true when rearing children, running a home, and keeping a marriage together. Sometimes, the last thing you feel like doing is being obedient to God. But that is what God expects of us. In John 14:23, Jesus tells us, "If anyone loves me, he will obey my teaching." But how do we do that? By surrendering our will to God.

The beauty of God's design for our lives is that when we give up ourselves, we are free to receive all that God has planned for us. The Bible tells us, "Whoever loses his life for my sake will find it" (Matthew 10:39). Through surrender we receive life.

The life God has for us is always much better for us than what we can do on our own. God tells us the reason in Isaiah 55:8: "My thoughts are not your thoughts, neither are your ways my ways." We often don't understand how God works. However, through many experiences in my life, I've learned that His ways are always best.

Oh, friend, tell God about your hurts, heartaches, and desires. His heart of compassion is eager to comfort you and give you guidance. Then trust His direction completely. Our heavenly Father knows best!

HIS WORD
"I know, my God, that you test the heart and are pleased with integrity. All these things have I given willingly and with honest intent" (1 Chronicles 29:17).

MY PART
"Holy Father, forgive my stubborn self-will. I know that You only want what is best for me. Help me daily to withstand the temptations that come my way so I may follow Your righteous plan instead. Give me the wisdom to discern Your perfect will. Amen."

MY STUDY
Psalm 119:1,2; 1 Thessalonians 4:7

A pastor and his wife were visiting their daughter at college. The parking lot at their hotel was full so the manager told them to park in a space reserved for handicapped guests. Thinking it would be okay, the pastor did as he was directed.

Rewards of Obedience

Some time later as they were leaving, the pastor noticed an older gentleman watching him. The man's eyes met his with a disgusted look. Then the pastor noticed the man's wife in a wheelchair. The pastor felt horrible, but he learned a good lesson from this situation: Don't trust what others tell you if it is contrary to what God would want you to do.

Friend, the Bible is clear. In Acts 5:29, Peter tells us, "We must obey God rather than men." Even when we receive instruction from a person in authority, we must weigh that against God's instructions. Are they in conflict? If so, then we must choose to obey God. He has given us many guidelines in His Word.

One of the instructions God has given us that we can apply to this situation is in James 4:17: "Anyone, then, who knows the good he ought to do and doesn't do it, sins." Sins are not only things that we do, but also things that we should have done but didn't do.

Sometimes doing the right thing is hard. It may put us in conflict with others who are not following God and don't understand our actions. But He expects us to do what we know to be right, no matter what.

The rewards of obedience are many. It gives us greater intimacy with God, credibility with others, and freedom from guilt. Obedience provides us with a clear conscience; it helps others God has placed in our path; it keeps us focused on Him rather than ourselves; and above all, it brings honor and glory to God.

HIS WORD
"The wicked man earns deceptive wages, but he who sows righteousness reaps a sure reward" (Proverbs 11:18).

MY PART
Think of a time when you had a conflict between an authority figure and God. How did you handle it? How would the principle you just learned have helped you? As you apply God's Word to your life, you will be blessed.

MY STUDY
Ruth 2:12;
Luke 12:41–48

Everyone suffers in life at one time or another, but it's our response to the suffering that matters. It determines whether we'll be bitter or better.

The biblical story of Ruth shows that she had every reason to be bitter—her husband, brother-in-law, and father-in-law had all died. She didn't have children, and she had no way to support herself. She could have gone home to her family, but she loved her mother-in-law, Naomi, and was committed to her. She told Naomi, "Where you go I will go, and where you stay I will stay. Your people will be my people and your God my God" (Ruth 1:16).

Ruth and Naomi moved to Bethlehem. There Ruth was considered an alien, but she worked hard in the barley fields to provide for herself and Naomi. In God's providence, she met Boaz, married him, and had a son. That child was King David's grandfather.

Ruth could have become bitter. Instead, she chose to use the circumstances in which she found herself to demonstrate the biblical virtues of faithfulness and love. With peace in her heart, she went where God led her, and He proved faithful.

What tragedies or unexpected events have occurred in your life, recently or in the past? How have you responded to them? If you have become bitter, dear friend, it's never too late to turn a hurtful or stressful circumstance into an opportunity for growth. God has given us free-will, so it is our choice to allow bitterness to take root or to allow God to heal our hurts and guide our lives.

Bitterness is destructive. Today, choose to recognize God's hand in your life. He is watching over you, and He makes no mistakes. No matter how your circumstances look at the moment, God is with you. It's your choice. Trusting Him will make you feel better, not bitter.

HIS WORD
"Above all else, guard your heart, for it is the wellspring of life" (Proverbs 4:23).

MY PART
"Lord Jesus, You know the bitterness I have in my heart. The wound is old and deep. I surrender it to You now, Lord. Please heal the pain so I may be free again to experience life as You want me to experience it. In Your name, amen."

MY STUDY
Ephesians 4:30–32; Isaiah 5:20

Leisha faced fear head-on. And she overcame it—with God's help.

She's a working mom whose life has been far from "normal." As a child, Leisha was physically and sexually abused. As a teenager, she placed her faith in Christ. It wasn't long before her young faith was tested.

He Cares for You

Leisha was attacked by a serial rapist. He was captured, and when his trial came around, she courageously faced her attacker on the witness stand—*twice*. He went to prison, but escaped—*twice*. And her worst nightmare came true: the rapist came after her again. Even though this was a terrifying experience for Leisha, she refused to let fear rule her life. Instead, she chose to trust God.

In the Scriptures, God says, "Do not fear, for I am with you...I will strengthen you and help you" (Isaiah 41:10). This is a wonderfully comforting promise from God.

Are there times when you are afraid? Perhaps the things you fear aren't as life-threatening as what Leisha faced. But just the same, God's promise holds true.

Fear is based on our lack of knowledge of the future. We want to know what is going to happen to us, but there is no way that we can know. Only God knows the future. We can trust God with our future because He loves us and has our best interests at heart.

You can remind yourself of this fact with 1 Peter 5:7. It says, "Cast all your anxiety on him because he cares for you." This verse does not leave any care to our own efforts. God provides for us in everything.

Dear friend, the Lord has proven Himself faithful to Leisha, and He will for you too! Confess *your* fear to the Lord today. Trust Him to care for you and protect you.

HIS WORD
"The LORD is my light and my salvation—whom shall I fear?" (Psalm 27:1).

MY PART
"All-powerful God, forgive me for being afraid. I know that You control everything and that not even a sparrow falls without Your notice. Help me to live each day wholly trusting in Your mighty power and wisdom. In Jesus' blessed name, amen."

MY STUDY
Nehemiah 4:14; 2 Timothy 1:7

One Monday morning, I awakened to news that a dear friend of mine had died. Although Ann had been quite ill, she had recovered and was so vibrant and active. I was not prepared for the news of her death. I was stunned and heartbroken.

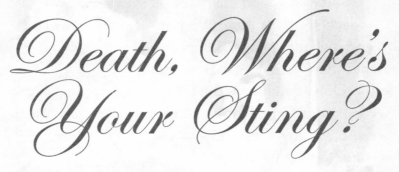

Death, Where's Your Sting?

By noon that same day, I received word of the death of one of my dearest friends—a woman I'd known and loved for more than forty years. Mrs. Atkinson was 103 years old. She'd lived a full and meaningful life, yet there is something profoundly sad about her death. I will never again hear her say, "Well, honey, I'm still here. God must have something for me to do."

Then later that week, I learned about the homegoing of a lifelong friend and classmate. She stood as my bridesmaid.

That unusual week has left me very thoughtful about the realities of life...and death.

The day after my friend Ann died, her young granddaughter said, "Mommy, what do you think grandmother is having for breakfast with Jesus this morning?"

We all smiled. The little girl grasped a reality that some of us as adults can easily miss. She knew her grandmother was gone, but she was still alive, in heaven with Jesus. She was in the presence of her dear Savior, enjoying the place that He'd prepared for her. I know this because it's what the Bible teaches. It's real.

Three of my friends experienced the blessed hope of heaven. The Lord Jesus Christ had gloriously appeared to them, and they were ready to meet Him.

My question to you is this: Are you ready?

Life is very brief. Before we know it, our years on this earth will come to an end. The most important thing that we can do in this short period of time is to prepare for eternity—eternity with God.

HIS WORD

"When the perishable has been clothed with the imperishable, and the mortal with immortality, then the saying that is written will come true: 'Death has been swallowed up in victory'" (1 Corinthians 15:54).

MY PART

If today were your last day to live, would you be ready? Do you know where you would spend eternity? My friend, you can know for certain. Turn to the back of the book to learn how you can place your heart in His hands and Begin Your Journey of Joy.

MY STUDY

Isaiah 25:8; Psalm 68:20

The Wise Heart

The fear of the Lord is the beginning of wisdom; all who follow his precepts have good understanding. To him belongs eternal praise.

PSALM 111:10

Never before in history has there been so much information available. It has been well said that "information is power, but only to those who know how to use it."

I am grateful for the marvelous grace of God in allowing me to meet so many knowledgeable and capable people. I never want to stop learning and filling my mind with information and ideas that will better equip me to share the gospel. As Bill and I have faced serious issues about his health and attempted to make wise decisions about treatment and medications, we have realized our total dependence on the wisdom that only God can give. There is great security in trusting God to illumine our minds and confirm His Word in our hearts.

Do you have any idea how many choices you made today? It would be impossible to accurately count. The many options available for everything from breakfast cereal to automobiles is staggering. It is easy to see why young people have such a difficult time choosing a career path.

When we seek God's wisdom and rest our heart securely in His hands, we have a solid foundation for our lives. We can rest in His promise: "If you want to know what God wants you to do, ask him, and he will gladly tell you, for he is always ready to give a bountiful supply of wisdom to all who ask him; he will not resent it" (James 1:5, TLB).

While on a speaking tour in Taiwan, we were given generous gifts by our hosts. My traveling partner was given a beautiful cloisonné vase.

Unfamiliar with the art of cloisonné, my friend had no appreciation for the treasure she had received. She had never witnessed the craftsmanship required to create her beautiful vase, never knew about the countless hours invested by many people who tediously designed, ground, sanded, and polished the vase.

His Treasure

She admitted the vase didn't quite complement her decor so she had tucked it safely in a closet!

Several weeks later, a catalog from an exclusive store arrived in her home. While browsing its pages, she found an exact replica of her vase—along with a hefty price tag. Immediately, the vase came out of hiding and into a prominent place in her living room. She has since absolutely fallen in love with this wonderful piece of artistry.

What changed? The value of the vase. When it was worthless in her eyes, she treated it as such. Once she discovered what people paid for such an item, she treated it with care and respect.

My friend's misunderstanding is not unlike misjudgments we make. But we can change. If we take a good, long look at the world and the people around us, we'll see them through the eyes of their Creator. Regardless of outward appearance, achievements, gifts, or abilities; regardless of where we've been or who we know, we are all His treasure. Therefore, we should treat each other with dignity and kindness.

Understanding this truth will also impact the way we see ourselves. When I'm discouraged over my own inadequacies and failures, when I consider areas of my life that aren't what I want them to be, I need to remember that my worth is not tied to those things. I am a treasure to the living God. So are you.

HIS WORD

"Rich and poor have this in common: The LORD is the Maker of them all" (Proverbs 22:2).

MY PART

Do you have anyone in your life that you're treating like an unwanted vase? Maybe you're treating yourself that way. You're worth so much more! We all are. Remember, God paid a supreme price for you and for me. He values you!

MY STUDY

Job 34:18,19; Matthew 10:29–31

The Bible tells us that Martha welcomed Jesus into her home for dinner. But she was so busy with her preparations for the guests that she didn't have time to sit and listen to Him. However, Mary, her sister, did take the time to listen intently to the Lord. Martha was not happy about this, and the Lord told her, "Martha, Martha, you are worried and upset about many things, but only one thing is needed" (Luke 10:38–41).

Mary and Martha

Can you relate to the story of Martha? Suzanne can. She has a hard time sitting still, too. The need to constantly be doing something is ever-present in her life. After learning about Martha, Suzanne wanted to make a change. So she posted a note that said, "Be Mary, not Martha!"

Then she tried to be Mary. She tried to sit quietly and listen to God, but it was difficult. Soon her mind was racing to her "to do" list. Even though her will wanted to be like Martha, the rest of her was not ready for it.

Finally, Suzanne realized that Jesus never told Martha to *be* Mary. He told her not to worry about the unimportant things. When Jesus came to visit Mary and Martha, the important thing was not the food and preparations. The important thing was that the Lord Jesus was preaching the gospel.

That's a great lesson for us all: We must not focus on the cares of this world. There is a time for everything. There is a time for taking care of worldly concerns—cooking, cleaning, etc. But our focus is always to be on the Lord. When He wants to meet with us, we must shut out all distractions.

Remember, the Christian life is a *relationship* with God. He cares about you and wants to spend time with you! Will you give your attention to Him?

HIS WORD

"One thing I ask of the LORD, this is what I seek: that I may dwell in the house of the LORD all the days of my life, to gaze upon the beauty of the LORD and to seek him in his temple" (Psalm 27:4).

MY PART

The next time you are worried or anxious, stop to consider if these things are really important. I can guarantee you that most, if not all, of them are not. Take some time to sit at Jesus' feet and listen. Your worries will quickly fade away.

MY STUDY

*Hosea 10:12;
1 John 2:15–17*

DAY 33

It's a temptation that confronts all of us. You know what you *should* do, but what you *want* to do is something entirely different.

Let me use a simple illustration to make a very serious point.

Good or Better

Let's say there's a world-class ice cream store near your home. Each time your car gets near that street, you have a little conversation with yourself that goes something like this:

"I think I'll stop and get some ice cream."

Another voice says, "You shouldn't have any. You don't need it."

"I love it; I really want some."

"You shouldn't have any. It's not good for you."

The voice saying you can't have any Praline Supreme makes you want it all the more. So you stop in and make your purchase.

As you leave the shop, you can still hear the voice saying, "You shouldn't be eating this." Something in you feels guilty, but you keep right on eating.

That's the illustration. Now, let's make the point.

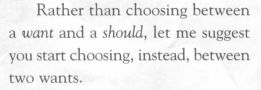

Rather than choosing between a *want* and a *should*, let me suggest you start choosing, instead, between two wants.

Do I want to get some ice cream? Or do I want to be healthy?

Which do I want more? It's not a choice of feeling guilty versus good. It's a matter of choosing between good and better.

That kind of thinking gives you freedom! When you drive by the ice cream store, you can extend a little grace to yourself.

So often I speak to women who have put themselves beneath a huge load of guilt. They're overwhelmed by all the self-imposed "shoulds" in life.

Remember, it's God's grace that gives us the freedom to be obedient to His will. In John 8:36, Jesus said, "If the Son sets you free, you will be free indeed."

Isn't that what we really *want*?

HIS WORD
"I have set before you life and death, blessings and curses. Now choose life, so that you and your children may live and that you may love the LORD your God, listen to his voice, and hold fast to him. For the LORD is your life" (Deuteronomy 30:19,20).

MY PART
Take time to think about how this applies to you. Are you bound by a strict set of artificial rules that you've made up yourself? Do they weigh you down and force you to react out of guilt more than a desire to make the best decision? Apply God's grace to these situations.

MY STUDY
Proverbs 4:25–27; Ephesians 6:7,8

At 43, Frank was diagnosed with an incurable form of cancer that spread from his legs to his lungs, spleen, and various parts of his body. Within days, Frank gave his life to Jesus—something his wife, Cathy, and his sons had prayed about for many years.

Make the Most of Today

Until now, Frank had been a stern and stoic father. He taught his three boys to be strong and tough. Only manly handshakes were exchanged at bedtime. He was better at giving advice than he was at listening.

God worked miraculously in Frank's life at a Family-Life Marriage Conference. He went home a changed man, husband, and dad.

Hugging and loving his sons became commonplace. He shared from his heart with the boys, cried with them, told them how proud he was of them, and how very much he loved them. He also became the listening, loving husband every wife dreams of.

His last four months were filled with laughter and good times with his family. Even though the cancer was overcoming his body, God gave him a good quality of life to the end.

Three weeks before Frank died, the boys' uncle encouraged them to write their dad a letter of love to ensure that nothing would go unsaid. Each boy read it to their dad and, together, son and father wept for the blessing they were to each other.

When Frank died, the boys were at his side. The family came to that moment with no regrets. They had the chance to prepare.

Many of us will not have that chance. We won't have advance warning when a loved one dies. Unfortunately, some of us will live the rest of our lives wishing we had a little more time—just one more chance.

Friend, you can't take back yesterday, and we aren't guaranteed tomorrow. Make the most of today! You won't regret you did!

HIS WORD

"Timothy has just now come to us from you and has brought good news about your faith and love. He has told us that you always have pleasant memories of us and that you long to see us, just as we also long to see you" (1 Thessalonians 3:6).

MY PART

Don't wait to tell your parents, your spouse, or your children how much they mean to you. Don't wait until tomorrow to make memories. Take time today to plan meaningful times with those you love.

MY STUDY

2 Samuel 1:26; Proverbs 3:3,4

J ulia had earned a Bible degree from a Christian college, and she attended church faithfully. But something was missing.

Over coffee with a friend, Julia shared her problem: "I just don't *feel* like I'm a Christian anymore. I don't *feel* like reading the Bible. I know I should, but I just don't."

Fact, Faith, Feeling

Her friend offered a simple illustration to try to help. She told her to picture a train with three cars. The engine represents *fact*—the truth of God and His Word. The coal car behind the engine represents *faith*—our trust in God and His Word. Finally, the caboose represents *feeling*—which is the result of our faith and obedience.

All three are important, but a train can run without its caboose. In the train of our spiritual life, our confidence must be in the only reliable engine—God and His Word. Feelings shouldn't pull us along. It's not that feelings don't exist, but we can't *depend* on our feelings to provide power for our lives.

Over the next two weeks, Julia started reading the Bible again and believing its truth. She prayed that the Holy Spirit would empower and direct her life. Julia's life began to take on a whole new meaning. She began rediscovering the truth about herself, about God, and about the world around her.

If you find yourself on a spiritual roller coaster, it's possible you're being pulled by the wrong engine! Turn to the Scripture and choose to rely on God's Word rather than your feelings.

Maybe you've been trying to live the Christian life on your own power and you, like Julia, *feel* defeated. Today, renew your commitment to God and quit relying on the caboose of feelings to power your train! Get into the habit of putting your faith in the facts, and the feelings will follow. It's simple, but life changing.

HIS WORD
"The LORD is good, a refuge in times of trouble. He cares for those who trust in him" (Nahum 1:7).

MY PART
"Lord Jesus, forgive me for trying to live the Christian life on my own power. I want Your Spirit to empower and direct me. From this point on, I will trust in You and Your Word and not my feelings. In Your holy name, amen."

MY STUDY
Psalm 125:1; Ephesians 1:18,19

According to the Department of Health and Human Services, 43 percent of adults suffer adverse health effects from stress.

No wonder the newsstands are lined with magazines that include articles on managing stress! These emphasize that eating well, getting adequate rest, exercising regularly, and maintaining friendships are all essential to coping with stress.

Relieving Stress

King David recognized that the greatest stress buster is a loving relationship with a sovereign God. In Psalm 37, he gives us this advice: "Trust in the LORD...Delight yourself in the LORD...Commit your way to the LORD ...Be still before the LORD and wait patiently for him; do not fret..." (vv. 3–7).

God understands our tendency to be worried and stressed about our lives. He extends His great compassion and mercy to us when we're burdened by life's demands. Philippians 4:6 says,

> Do not be anxious about anything, but in everything, by prayer and petition, with thanksgiving, present your requests to God. And the peace of God, which tran-

scends all understanding, will guard your hearts and your minds in Christ Jesus.

Reading God's Word for even ten or fifteen minutes at the beginning of a busy day helps me put everything in the right perspective. I'm reminded of what's important to God—my character and my trust in Him—not what's important to me.

My mind will revert back to worry unless I am persistently praying. At the beginning of the day, I like to tell God about every activity and important relationship. As the day goes on, every time I start to be concerned about something, I cast my cares upon God.

Begin each day by reading His Word and by praying. God didn't intend for you to be ineffective due to worrying. He wants to use you, and He wants you to experience His peace as you walk closely with Him.

HIS WORD
"Therefore let everyone who is godly pray to you while you may be found; surely when the mighty waters rise, they will not reach him" (Psalm 32:6).

MY PART
Set aside a time each day for you to connect with God through Bible study and prayer. Pick a quiet place where you won't be distracted or interrupted. Make it a priority in your life. It will relieve stress, keep you close to your heavenly Father, and set you free.

MY STUDY
Jonah 2:1–6; Matthew 11:28–30

When my young friend Kara became engaged, she was thrilled with the prospect of marrying the man she loves. Kara read numerous wedding planners, grilled her married friends for ideas, and used every spare moment thinking about how to make her wedding day special.

Focus on Him

Instead of being satisfied as her plans fell into place, she felt more and more empty and unfulfilled. *What happened?* she thought. *Where have I gone wrong? I thought this was supposed to be a fulfilling experience.*

It finally dawned on her that during this time of transition, she had lost sight of God. Caught up in the details of planning the big day and focusing solely on her new life with her mate, Kara had taken her eyes off Jesus.

My friend, God can use transition times in our lives to teach us how much we need Him. As our earthly props are removed, we find ourselves spiritually lacking.

It's an uncomfortable place to be. It's frustrating, confusing, and lonely to be at the end of ourselves. But that's exactly where we need to be to get back on track with God.

When Kara realized that her preoccupation with wedding plans had caused her to lose sight of God, she knew something had to change. She confessed to God that she'd gone her own way, not pursuing Him as her first priority.

Let me ask you: Have your props been knocked out from under you? Have you taken your eyes off the Lord? Well, there's hope! You can tell God exactly where you are —the stresses you face, the challenges to make it through the day. You can confess anything that might be keeping you from a close relationship with Him.

Satan would love nothing more than to distract you! He would have total victory if He could get you to take your eyes off Jesus. Don't let him.

HIS WORD
"To love [God] with all your heart, with all your understanding and with all your strength, and to love your neighbor as yourself is more important than all burnt offerings and sacrifices" (Mark 12:33).

MY PART
"Heavenly Father, I confess my lack of love for You. You are the only One who can fill the emptiness and instill my life with meaning and purpose. While I am doing good things, keep me focused on You alone. In my life, Lord, be glorified. In Jesus' name I pray. Amen."

MY STUDY
Proverbs 19:21; Deuteronomy 6:5

What is most important in your life? Have you ever seriously thought about this question? For many the answer would be power, position, satisfaction, or happiness.

Eternal Investment

I love what Corrie ten Boom, a survivor of the holocaust, once said about the elusive "treasures" of this world: "The more firmly I hold on to something, the more it hurts when God has to pry my fingers away from it!"

Jesus put it best when He asked this probing question in Matthew 16:26, "What good will it be for a man if he gains the whole world, yet forfeits his soul?"

Yes, we all have to earn a living. We must provide for our families. But the greatest investment we can make is not on Wall Street. It's in the life of another. It's in loving, teaching, and caring for your children, your spouse, your parents. It's in reaching out to your friends, neighbors, and colleagues with the love of Jesus. It's putting their concerns above the financial investments or possessions we own.

Sometimes that's by directly sharing the gospel message. Sometimes it's by listening to a broken heart, praying together, providing a meal or an hour of baby-sitting. Other times it's by going for an ice cream cone during a moment of discouragement, or giving a comforting hug.

Those are the attitudes and actions that will develop character, godliness, love, compassion, and joy in your life. Those are the characteristics that Christ modeled throughout His life on earth and the only factors that matter in light of eternity. The rest will fade away.

Dear friend, where is your treasure? On what do you have a tight-fisted grip? What is most important in *your* life? Once you know the answer to that question, the real work of living the Christian life, day to day, can begin.

HIS WORD

"[The LORD] will be the sure foundation for your times, a rich store of salvation and wisdom and knowledge; the fear of the LORD is the key to this treasure" (Isaiah 33:6).

MY PART

"Lord Jesus, forgive me for not making You the most important person in my life. Show me how I need to re-prioritize my life. I want You to be first above everything, and reflect that in my attitudes and actions. In Your matchless name, amen."

MY STUDY

Proverbs 15:6
1 Peter 1:17–19

Many people never think they will end up in a homeless shelter. Edmond was one such person. After the construction company where he had worked folded, Edmond worked part-time at a grocery store while his wife, Shirley, cleaned houses. Even so, they soon started falling behind on house payments.

Infinite Security

Then one night, faulty wiring started a fire in their house. Two days later, their furniture was stolen.

In the months that followed, Shirley and their six daughters stayed with relatives while Edmond tried to fix the house. The damage was beyond repair, and the six children were too much for Shirley's mother. Swallowing his pride, Edmond agreed to try the shelter, but only for a few weeks.

Feeling ashamed, Edmond withdrew. The only prayer he could mutter was, "Lord, get me out of here." Edmond felt that all eyes were on him wherever he went, as if he wore a scarlet "H" for "homeless."

Eventually, Edmond found a job with a landscaping company, but it was a long time before they were freed from their financial woes and could leave the shelter.

One night, Edmond opened his Bible and realized he hadn't been praying for help—only for an escape. Clutching his Bible, he prayed, "I am here, God. And so are you. Please help me."

Edmond's shame began to dissolve. God's presence made the shelter a home. He needed to make himself available to God *no matter where he and his family lived.*

Though they now have a home of their own, they learned some invaluable lessons. Above all, they realized that the eternal is far more significant and secure than the temporal.

My friend, the temporal things of this world will all pass away. Place your faith in the infinite security of eternal things—God's things. He will never let you down.

HIS WORD

"Now we know that if the earthly tent we live in is destroyed, we have a building from God, an eternal house in heaven, not built by human hands" (2 Corinthians 5:1).

MY PART

Are you feeling hopeless today? Maybe your soul is restless or circumstances have left you questioning if God is really there. Friend, wherever you might be today, He is our shelter, our refuge. Rest in the promise of God's presence, knowing your heart is in His hands.

MY STUDY

Psalm 23:6; Deuteronomy 33:27

At 42, Bob was a husband, father, and pastor. Not too long ago, he was golfing with two doctors, both ten years his senior. He asked them this question: "What would you tell a guy like me about the next ten years—the years between 42 and 52?"

Your Gift to the World

The doctors discussed this thoughtful question. They found agreement on two main points. First, you should recognize it's unlikely you will make a great contribution to the world at large. Second, realize that the best legacy you will leave is in the lives of your children.

Friend, I believe all of us can see the wisdom in these words. Only a handful of people will truly impact the entire world, but there is more to the story. We have access to the One who *has* impacted the entire world— Jesus Christ. And each of us has our own "world" of influence—people with whom we have contact day to day. Through Christ's power we can have a positive effect on their lives.

If you are a parent, you know that the most important lives you will affect are those of your children. In Psalm 127, we're encouraged to build godly homes. Then we're reminded that children are a gift and blessing from God. Verse 3 tells us, "Sons are a heritage from the Lord, children a reward from him." We need to cherish the blessing of children. We are responsible for modeling Christ in their lives so that they may come to know Him personally and follow His will for their lives.

Dear friend, tenderly care for your children. Invest your time and energy in them. Teach them the Word of God. The most effective way to do this is to model Christ through your life in your day-to-day activities. Your children will be your greatest contribution to the world!

HIS WORD
"If any of you lacks wisdom, he should ask God, who gives generously to all without finding fault, and it will be given to him" (James 1:5).

MY PART
"Father, give me a wise heart as I consider my personal goals and ambitions along with the responsibilities, challenges, and rewards of rearing children. Help me to realize that childrearing requires only about one-third of my life, then I have two-thirds of my life to devote to personal pursuits. In Your merciful name, amen."

MY STUDY
Deuteronomy 32:46,47; Psalm 34:11

DAY 41

By nature, we are impatient. We rush through life, working hard to accomplish a goal, to move forward, to better our position.

I'm reminded of that every time I land at an airport. I can hardly wait to unbuckle my seat belt. I hurry out of my seat only to stand and wait uncomfortably in the aisle for another five minutes until the door is opened.

Slowing Down

We're always in a hurry to get ahead! But I'm convinced that much of the joy in life is found not in finishing or in getting ahead, but in the process of living and growing.

The late Erma Bombeck did so much to make us laugh, to help us see things from another perspective, and to help us realize that life, at times, cannot be taken too seriously.

I remember something she wrote long ago:

If I had my life to live over again, I would have waxed less and listened more.

Instead of wishing away nine months of pregnancy and complaining about the shadows over my feet, I'd have cherished every minute of it and realized the wonderment growing inside me would be my only chance in life to assist God in a miracle.

I would have cried and laughed less while watching television… and more while watching life …There would have been more I love yous…more I'm sorry… more I'm listening.

But mostly, given another shot at life, I would seize every minute of it…and never give that minute back until there was nothing left of it.

Life only passes once. We cannot fix the past. We can find forgiveness, certainly, but we cannot change history.

Dear friend, let's live every moment doing good under God's power. You'll have a more joyful life.

HIS WORD

"You have made known to me the path of life; you will fill me with joy in your presence, with eternal pleasures at your right hand" (Psalm 16:11).

MY PART

Are you constantly in a hurry? Friend, slow down. Take time to enjoy the process of living and growing in your faith. "Lord, remind me to take time to see the beauty of Your creation and to take time to love those who are dear to me."

MY STUDY

Ecclesiastes 3:1–8; Romans 14:17,18

The late pastor Ray Stedman told the story of how he worked his way through seminary as a mortuary attendant on the night shift.

Dr. Stedman discovered that the undertakers had special connections with clothing manufacturers. Since they bought large quantities, they were able to buy dark blue funeral suits rather inexpensively.

Issues of the Heart

Just beginning his preaching career, Dr. Stedman needed a new suit. So he asked the owners of the mortuary if he could buy a suit from them for himself. They agreed, and he was fitted for one. He soared with enthusiasm. He thought he'd gotten a real bargain!

Well, the next Sunday morning he put on his new suit. He brushed down the pleat of the pants, then the sleeves of the coat. He looked proudly into the mirror.

When he picked up his wallet and keys, his pride quickly turned to dismay. He searched in vain for a place to put them. This wonderful, handsome new suit had *no pockets!* The suit was made for a dead man, a man who didn't need pockets!

That's pretty funny, but it's true. I once heard someone say, "I never saw a hearse pulling a U-Haul."

Even though we know that things are temporary, our lives are consumed at times with accumulating them. Our attention gets focused on some possession we want to acquire. Aren't there times you find yourself thinking, *I have to have that purse, those draperies, that food processor, that dress?* Those *things* seem so important, more important than they are.

Friend, things don't last forever, and in the long run, they don't satisfy. Issues of the heart are what really matter.

Are you investing your time, energy, and money in what will last forever? You are when you read God's Word, enjoy fellowship with Christian friends, or reach out to nonbelievers. You are when you serve. These are eternal investments. What lasts for eternity is what's in the heart, not the pocket.

HIS WORD
"Seek first his kingdom and his righteousness, and all these things will be given to you as well" (Matthew 6:33).

MY PART
"Heavenly Father, please forgive me for placing my pursuit of possessions before my pursuit of You. I want You alone to be the focus of my life. I want to invest myself completely in Your will, to serve You. In Jesus' righteous name, amen."

MY STUDY
Psalm 86:11; Jeremiah 24:7

DAY 43

When stepping into an elevator, I'm always amazed at how silent things become. Aren't you?

You step into that little cubicle with several people, and when the door glides shut, there's a synchronized code of silence. Everyone turns to face the doors and looks up to watch the lighted numbers change.

No one moves! No one seems to breathe. It's a rare moment when someone shares a genuine greeting and exchange inside an elevator.

This experience is a snapshot of American life. The closer we get to one another, the more silent many people become. The more heated and controversial the issues, the more discrete Christians become—not wanting to draw any personal attention.

This concerns me. Nothing will kill the impact of Christian influence more than apathy and silence!

Dr. Philip Zimbardo, a professor of psychology, wrote an article for *Psychology Today* called "The Age of Indifference." He said this: "I know of no more potent killer than isolation. There is no more destructive influence on physical and mental health than the isolation of you from me and of us from them...The devil's strategy for our times is to trivialize human existence in a number of ways: by isolating us from one another while creating the delusion that the reasons are time pressures, work demands, or anxieties."

My friend, I wonder if you've begun to buy into the lie. Have you become isolated in your perspective on social concerns, whether they are local or national? Have you grown dependent on others to express your viewpoints?

Please know how critical it is for you to remain engaged, involved, and outspoken in your Christian views! Those who do not believe in your values are vocal and are influencing others to their way of thinking. Freedoms are meaningless unless we exercise them.

Be a light to a dark world.

HIS WORD

"When the righteous thrive, the people rejoice; when the wicked rule, the people groan" (Proverbs 29:2).

MY PART

Are you informed about current events that affect you and your fellow citizens? You can become involved in social issues through various organizations, share your views with your government representatives, and fast and pray with other concerned Christians.

MY STUDY

Isaiah 33:5,6; Acts 17:26–28

How we spend our time says so much about us. It says, *This is where my heart is. This is what's important to me.*

In her mid-twenties, Sarah Dunn Clarke spent many hours on an "elaborate" decoration for her house. When it was finished, this question penetrated her heart: *What are you doing to decorate your heavenly home?* That question changed the course of her life.

Make Your Time Count

She began to understand the sacred value of time and how she was spending God's precious time on things that wouldn't last. He began to show Sarah it was the *souls* of men and women that were important.

A few years later, Sarah moved to Chicago. One day while preparing for yet another social event, she said "no." Instead, she put on casual clothes and began visiting poor and needy families.

She wrote this: "In ministering to their needs I found such real soul satisfaction—such a consciousness of God's approval—that I was at once convinced my mission in life had been revealed."

That was in the mid-1800s, Civil War days. Times were desperate. Sarah and a few others founded a mission Sunday school, a little haven where children could be children. She lovingly taught them about Jesus Christ and His love.

In her late thirties, Sarah married a businessman in real estate. He didn't share her passion to reach the poor and needy. But some years later, God changed his heart. He and Sarah began the Pacific Garden Mission, which continues to reach the homeless and poor.

Ask yourself, *Where am I spending my time? Is it counting for eternity?* Then, ask God to make your time count for Him.

Like George and Sarah Clarke, *you* can make a difference in people's lives. A difference that leads others to Him and gives you "real soul satisfaction."

HIS WORD
"Command them to do good, to be rich in good deeds, and to be generous and willing to share. In this way they will lay up treasure for themselves as a firm foundation for the coming age, so that they may take hold of the life that is truly life" (1 Timothy 6:18,19).

MY PART
Do you want "real soul satisfaction"? Make this commitment: "Compassionate Father, I am willing to spend my life doing Your will and making a difference in people's lives. I choose the souls of men over the pleasures of this world. In Jesus' name, amen."

MY STUDY
1 Samuel 12:24; Proverbs 27:1

hile waiting for a friend at a bookstore café, Julie faced three temptations. She browsed through the mugs on sale, thinking that a special, new mug would give her a happy, full experience of drinking coffee. But she realized coffee and mugs don't meet her needs. God does.

Life to the Full

Next, she saw many secular books and magazines. Reading them would bring her up to date with this ever-changing culture. That would make her more effective in sharing the gospel message with others.

Well, she recognized that wasn't at all true. She didn't need all that information. Besides, she'd always be tempted to read them instead of her Bible.

Julie made this observation: "God gives us what we need in order to influence the people He's placed in our lives. If I don't stay in the Word of God, which is my spiritual food, I will have nothing of lasting substance to offer."

The third temptation came as she watched a young couple in love. A successful relationship might make her happy. That, too, was a lie. She knew that only a relationship with Christ would bring lasting love and fulfillment.

This is the point: There's absolutely nothing wrong with any of these things. What's wrong is that the world tells us we *need* all of these things to have a satisfying and fulfilling life. That is *not* true.

Jesus said, "I have come that they may have life, and have it to the full" (John 10:10).

He is our example. When He faced forty days of temptation by Satan, Jesus chose not to sin, but rather to quote Scripture. Don't believe the lies that the world tells you. Friend, knowing Jesus, praying, and memorizing Scripture are your best weapons against temptation and the only way to have true fulfillment.

HIS WORD
"Submit yourselves, then, to God. Resist the devil, and he will flee from you. Come near to God and he will come near to you" (James 4:7,8).

MY PART
Begin memorizing the truths of God's Word today. When you're tempted, go to God immediately. Quote the verses you have memorized (a good one is 1 Corinthians 10:13). If possible, leave the situation that is tempting you. Call a friend. Talk and pray with her until the temptation passes.

MY STUDY
Genesis 3:1–3; Psalm 119:151,152

My friend Luci Swindoll tells the story of learning to tithe. "Tithe" sounds like an old-fashioned word. The Bible talks about bringing our "tithes and offerings" to contribute to the work of God. A tithe is defined as a tenth of one's income.

Our Privilege

Luci grew up in a Christian home. Her parents were faithful to tithe their income. When Luci became an adult, she struggled with tithing. She was always generous and wanted to give to the cause of Christ, but she was nervous about committing a full tenth of her income. As a single, independent adult, she was solely responsible for herself. She didn't want to take any chances.

As she got older, she wondered if she was doing the right thing—giving only occasionally when she had extra money or giving only a limited amount. One day she asked her brother, Chuck, what he thought she should do.

Chuck Swindoll said to her, "Oh, Sis, by all means, you should always tithe."

"I'm afraid I'll run out of money," she responded.

"No, Sis," Chuck said, "you'll *never* run out…Don't give just ten percent, either. Give more."

"How about eleven?"

"That's great!"

That was many years ago. Luci took Chuck at his word that she'd never run out. Since then she's given an increasing percentage to the work of Christ and other charitable causes. She *delights* in doing this. Not only that, she's never been more financially secure.

God has given us the incomparable privilege of being involved in bringing His love and forgiveness to the entire world. God could certainly come up with other ways to finance the work of His kingdom, but He wants to involve you and me.

If you've never been involved, take it from Luci Swindoll, Chuck, or me. Take it from God Himself. When you tithe, God will bless you.

HIS WORD

"'Bring the whole tithe into the storehouse, that there may be food in my house. Test me in this,' says the LORD Almighty, 'and see if I will not throw open the floodgates of heaven and pour out so much blessing that you will not have room enough for it'" (Malachi 3:10).

MY PART

My friend, do you tithe? It's not about the money; it's about putting God first in every area of your life and trusting that He will provide for your needs. He will prove faithful. Test Him.

MY STUDY

Proverbs 3:9,10; 2 Corinthians 9:6–9

Matt and Rhonda had a "typical" middle-class family—nice home and lifestyle, two cars, two children, and two incomes, which meant two parents working full-time.

Simplify

But life was moving too quickly for them. Their schedule was keeping them from being with their children. Rhonda remembers making every effort to be there for them, but she was struggling to keep it all together. As this family grew in their Christian faith, one idea began to stir in each of their hearts: their family should be a higher priority than a comfortable lifestyle.

In the spring of 1996, Rhonda told Matt she believed God wanted her to be home—immediately. Matt struggled over Rhonda's decision to leave her successful occupational therapy practice. Her job provided sixty-one percent of their income. "We bought into the lie that a family can't make it without two incomes," Matt says.

As Matt left to attend a golf tournament, God worked on his heart. Matt sensed God assuring him that if he trusted Him with this matter, He'd provide. So Matt told Rhonda it was okay to leave her job. He said that with God's help, they were going to make it on one income.

The decisions they made were difficult, but Matt and Rhonda couldn't be happier. They now encourage others to follow God's plan. They have lived on both sides of the fence, and there's no question that they are where God wants them.

Oh dear friend, I'm so encouraged by their willingness to make lifestyle changes to simplify their lives. I'm even more encouraged that they listened to what God was telling them and obeyed.

What's right for one family is not necessarily right for another, but what's important is letting God set your priorities. Let Him provide the plan and the pattern for you. Ask Him and He'll show you. You can be sure of that!

HIS WORD

"Better one handful with tranquillity than two handfuls with toil and chasing after the wind" (Ecclesiastes 4:6).

MY PART

"All-knowing heavenly Father, forgive me for setting my own agenda. I want You alone to guide the priorities of my life. Give me wisdom to discern Your will in all I do. In Your Son's precious name, Amen."

MY STUDY

Psalm 119:73; 1 Thessalonians 4:11,12

As a child, Dwayne placed his trust in Christ. "As I grew older, if anyone had asked me, I would've proclaimed that I loved the Lord, and that He was the most important person in my life," Dwayne said.

But something happened to Dwayne that happens to many Christians. It subtly robs Christians of their joy and a vibrant walk with God.

Welcome Back

Dwayne said, "Over the years, in very subtle ways, other people and things had become more important to me than my relationship with Jesus Christ. Christianity has always been a part of me, but not *all* of me."

Dwayne gradually put school, women, career, money, and other activities ahead of God. As he did, his relationship with God suffered.

Later, a restless gnawing on his conscience developed. Dwayne tried to keep God in his family by taking them to church and leading them in prayers. But he was doing little more than just going through the motions.

A friend told Dwayne that he was living what some call a "carnal" life. In other words, Dwayne had placed his trust in Christ, but he wasn't living like it. He was living his life *his* way, not as God would have him live it. Dwayne began to get the picture.

Driving home after that conversation, Dwayne stopped his car, bowed his head, confessed his sin, and asked God to forgive him. Then He invited Christ, in the power of the Holy Spirit, to resume control of his life. God answered, and Dwayne became a changed man.

Friend, many of us wander away from God. One step at a time, we walk away. But God said in His Word that He will *never* leave us. He waits patiently and quietly for us to return. When we do, He forgives us and lovingly welcomes us back.

HIS WORD
"I the LORD do not change . . . Return to me, and I will return to you" (Malachi 3:6,7).

MY PART
"Dear Father, I need You. I acknowledge that I've been directing my own life. As a result, I've sinned against You. Thank You for forgiving my sin. I now invite You to direct my life. Fill me with Your Holy Spirit. Help me to walk in His power. As an expression of my faith, I thank You. In Jesus' name, amen."

MY STUDY
Psalm 80:3; 1 Peter 2:25

A missionary had a great and immediate need for a large sum of money. The letter expressing the need was read aloud at a luncheon for Christian women. The president of the organization asked the guest speaker to lead in prayer, asking God to provide the funds.

Let Them Go

To her surprise, the speaker said, "No, I won't pray for God to meet the needs of this missionary. But I'll tell you what I will do. I'll give every dime of cash I have in my pockets and place it on the table. I'm asking each of you to do the same. If we don't have four thousand dollars, then I'll pray for God to meet their needs...I challenge you to give what you have now. No credit cards, no checks."

Then he took all of his cash out of his wallet and pockets, and placed it on the table. Though a bit reluctant, three hundred luncheon guests followed suit. Wallets and purses were opened and emptied. When the cash was counted, it was well above four thousand dollars.

Then the speaker said, "You see, we didn't need to pray that God would provide the resources. They were already there. *We just had to let them go."*

Isn't that true? Many times we hear about the needs of missionaries or families in our churches and neighborhoods. We say we'll pray for God to provide. But what we really need to do is ask God to help us let go of our own wallets, our own resources.

When three hundred people gave what they had, it was more than enough to cover the great need. That's the way God works.

The next time you hear of a need, consider your resources and how you can help. Ask God to help you know what to do. Then do it. You'll be a blessing to others and glorify God.

HIS WORD

"Just as you excel in everything—in faith, in speech, in knowledge, in complete earnestness and in your love for us—see that you also excel in this grace of giving" *(2 Corinthians 8:7).*

MY PART

"Great Provider God, You have blessed my life abundantly, materially, and spiritually. I know that it isn't the amount that is important, but the heart of the giver that matters to you. Help me to give willingly and cheerfully. In Your Son's holy name, amen."

MY STUDY

Proverbs 11:24,25; Jeremiah 22:16

Nancy heard the tour guide say, "On Tuesday morning we're going to the leper colony." Fear gripped her heart. *No way!* she thought. She'd signed up for a short-term mission trip to West Africa, but nowhere on the schedule had she read "leper colony." She was terrified.

Counting for Eternity

As the team was preparing to leave for the leper colony, she felt a little embarrassed, even silly, for not going. But she also felt safer, more secure, and less afraid by staying put. Then the missionary said he didn't know if these lepers had ever heard the gospel.

Suddenly, Paul's words in Acts 20:24 gripped her heart: "I consider my life worth nothing to me, if only I may finish the race and complete the task the Lord Jesus has given me—the task of testifying to the gospel of God's grace."

In that instant, God showed Nancy that there is something greater than her own personal safety. If she held her life dear to herself, she would never finish the course and the ministry God had for her. That ministry, she believed, was to declare the gospel of the grace of God. Suddenly she felt compelled to join the group.

That morning, through an interpreter, she shared the gospel with a small group of lepers. God met with them in a special way and almost all received Christ. Nancy was thrilled to participate in what God was doing. And to think, she almost missed out on that joyous occasion because she was afraid!

Since that mission trip, Nancy has faced fear and insecurity, but she's held God's hand and kept going, reaping great rewards and joy. She's experienced the power of God's grace. She says, "When life comes down to the bottom line, I want mine to have counted for all eternity."

Dear friend, you can make your race count for eternity.

HIS WORD

"This is what the Lord has commanded us: 'I have made you a light for the Gentiles, that you may bring salvation to the ends of the earth'" *(Acts 13:47).*

MY PART

Oh dear friend, don't be content with your own salvation. Be willing to take the gospel message to others. Start by praying for one person you can talk with about Christ. Read through an evangelistic booklet with them. Help them understand how to put their faith in Jesus Christ. Sharing Him with others will change your life. And their eternity.

MY STUDY

Psalm 97:11,12; Isaiah 51:4–6

n Psalm 42, it says, "As the deer
pants for streams of water, so my soul pants for you, O
God. My soul thirsts for God, for the living God" (vv.
1,2).

The psalmist, inspired by God, compares himself to
a beautiful and swift deer, which can sprint through the
forest. But deer tire quickly and need to be refreshed
with water throughout the day. He didn't compare himself with a camel, which is slow and walks through the
desert for days without water.

As the Deer

We take time during the day to *physically* refresh our
bodies with food and water, with exercise and sleep. But
we need spiritual refreshing as well. Because God has
fashioned us to be like deer, we need to have this time
of renewal, not only daily, but many times throughout
the day.

What seems to be depleting your spiritual resources?
You want to be an attentive, ever-present parent. You
want to be a loving, supportive wife. You want to be a
faithful, efficient employee. You want to be a loyal, caring friend. There are so many areas that demand your

time and energy. It is very easy to suddenly find yourself exhausted—physically, emotionally, and spiritually.

How do we get refreshed spiritually? By talking with God and reading His Word. The Bible gives us a simple, yet life-changing direction in 1 Thessalonians 5:17: "Pray continually." This verse instructs us to keep an open line of communication with God. God gives us wisdom to deal with each situation we encounter throughout the day. He guides us with His Spirit.

Spending time in God's Word is also important. Deuteronomy 8:3 tells us, "Man does not live on bread alone but on every word that comes from the mouth of the LORD." The Bible is God's unchanging Word to His creation. It gives us spiritual nourishment to feed our hungry soul.

Seek God daily. He'll refresh you as nothing else can.

HIS WORD

"Jesus declared, 'I am the bread of life. He who comes to me will never go hungry, and he who believes in me will never be thirsty'" (John 6:35).

MY PART

Take time out of your busy schedule to be alone with God. Let those around you know how important and necessary this time is. Do all that you can to always keep your day's most important appointment. God will give you the energy you need to face the day.

MY STUDY

Psalm 63:1; Isaiah 26:8

once heard a story of two pranksters who played a trick on a store manager. They decided to switch the price tags on various items displayed on the shelves.

After hours, they lurked down each of the aisles. Before long, mink coats carried tags of $5 and cotton blouses were $3,500. Tuxedos were $2.50 and men's neckties were $900.

True Value

After the store opened the next morning, it wasn't long before customers filled the check-out lines. Predictably, the manager found no humor in this prank and hurried to make things right.

This incident illustrates a reality in life. It's easy for us to devalue those things that are of tremendous worth while squandering our time, energy, and money on things that are of relatively little value.

We overlook the treasure of those people we hold dear and invest instead in bigger cars, better technology, and more possessions.

Let me ask you: Has someone played a trick on you? Are you allowing the price tags to be switched on the very things you hold most dear? What are you trading for these valuables today?

What about those things you can live without, possessions that come and go, that rust and wear out? Are they treated like they are your real treasures? Don't be deceived. We all fall into this trap and need to be reminded to put first things first.

Do you know what will help you more than anything else to keep your priorities in order? Nothing will keep you on track any more than a consistent walk with God— filled daily with His Spirit.

Viewing the world through Spirit-filled eyes will allow you to know the true value of the things around you. Then you won't be fooled when you are tempted to switch the price tags.

HIS WORD

"Wisdom is more precious than rubies, and nothing you desire can compare with her" (Proverbs 8:11).

MY PART

Dear friend, stop, look around you, and listen. What would you miss the most if it were taken from you? Make a list of those things you would define as valuable. Are the things of eternity high on your list? Regularly review this list to remind yourself of what's truly important.

MY STUDY

Ecclesiastes 2:26; 1 Peter 2:4–6

The cold Chicago Sunday began as it always had for the Mokry family. Ace and Marj went to church, then prepared for a relaxing afternoon with their family. After lunch, they enjoyed a lazy afternoon, sitting in front of the warm hearth, occasionally stoking the fire.

Treasures in Heaven

Then someone thought they smelled smoke. Ace headed for the garage, thinking he ought to at least check out the concern. When he opened the door, a huge fireball surged over his head. Billows of thick smoke were sucked into the house.

Everyone needed to get out—fast! Within seconds, flames engulfed the house, turning their afternoon of delight into an inferno of disaster.

The fire engines quickly arrived, but it was too late. From the front lawn, Ace and Marj watched a lifetime of dreams and memories be destroyed.

Dear friend, it may not be a fire on a quiet Sunday afternoon or the loss of your earthly possessions. But every family will confront times of difficulty, times when flames of destruction will come through the back door—a complete surprise.

God never promises life will be without difficulty. That's why it's essential to be grounded in His Word and in touch with what's most important to Him. Only then can we know the kind of peace the Mokrys felt when the fire struck their home. Their earthly treasures were gone, but they had an overwhelming sense that what mattered most to them could not be destroyed. Their treasure is in heaven.

The Mokry family had built their lives on the trustworthiness of God and His Word. Nothing in this world could take that away. Not only did they survive, but God and His Word gave them peace.

God can do the same thing for you. What family crisis are you facing right now? Keep your eyes focused on God.

HIS WORD

"The earth is the LORD's, and everything in it, the world, and all who live in it" (Psalm 24:1).

MY PART

Perhaps you will encounter disease, financial disaster, or an enemy threatening the welfare of your family. Make it a practice to talk about the goodness of God to your family and recount specific ways you have experienced His guidance and protection. Encourage your family to openly express their awareness of God's trustworthiness. Recognizing Him in the little things prepares us to see Him when major struggles occur.

MY STUDY

Isaiah 45:6,7; Philippians 4:11–13

Have you ever had something happen in your life that put everything in perspective for you? Judy did. Here is her story.

It was a busy, yet exciting time. Judy was preparing for a relaxing vacation on a cruise ship. As she checked off her long "to do" list, the phone rang. Her husband and two sons had been in a terrible car accident.

Simplicity

Her boys were going to be alright, but her husband had been very seriously hurt. He suffered twenty-two broken bones, and for a while the doctors weren't sure he would live. Thankfully, he did survive and in time recovered fully.

Since the accident, Judy has often thought about how simple she used to think her life was. Now, she was discovering simplicity had new meaning. When life had suddenly become a question of survival, few things seemed truly important. All the peripheral issues that she was concerned about from day to day became insignificant.

So what did Judy discover was *truly* important to her? Four things: the Lord, His Word, His people, and the precious time she had with her family. Everything else fell way down on the list.

In Matthew 22:37–39, Jesus tells us what He considers to be truly important: "Love the Lord your God with all your heart and with all your soul and with all your mind …Love your neighbor as yourself." Loving God first and then loving others are the two greatest commandments that He gave us. These are simple commands that, if followed, will have a profound impact on your life and the world around you.

Friend, what's important to you? Does your lifestyle reflect this perspective? Don't wait for something catastrophic to happen to start living the way God wants you to live. Don't be burdened with the cares of this world, but be set free because of the great love God has shown you for all eternity. Start right now.

HIS WORD
"Whom have I in heaven but you? And earth has nothing I desire besides you" (Psalm 73:25).

MY PART
"Heavenly Father, the one true God, thank You for Your unconditional love for me; for Your Word given for my benefit; for Your people who inspire and support me; and for the family You have given me to love and care for. In Jesus' wonderful name, amen."

MY STUDY
Deuteronomy 30:6; 1 Corinthians 8:6

Diagnosed with breast cancer, Jane declined chemotherapy to treat it. It would have harmed her unborn child. She also declined a doctor's suggestion of abortion.

Baby Jessica was born healthy. But two years later, Jane tragically lost her battle with cancer. She left behind her husband, Todd, and two dear children.

Sacrifice

Todd wrote, "Scripture says 'greater love has no one than this, that he lay down his life for his friends.' And Jane courageously showed us that type of love by giving up her life for our daughter—a sacrificial act of obedience to God and His Word, done with joy, peace, and contentment."

What a sad, but incredibly special story! Jane is a perfect example of the kind of love Jesus often spoke of—unconditional, sacrificial love. Jesus demonstrated His love for us when He suffered and died on the cross for our sin.

Oh, friend, we may never have to die for another. But God does call us to daily give up our lives, our selfish desires—willingly, obediently, even joyfully. In Luke

9:23, Jesus tells us, "If anyone would come after me, he must deny himself and take up his cross daily and follow me."

Sometimes denying ourselves means not taking the easy way out. Let's look at Jane's example again. If she were thinking only of herself, she would have had the chemotherapy or the abortion. Her life could have gone on for many more years. But Jane knew that God did not want her to do those things because the resulting death would have been against His law. Instead, she placed her trust in Him. Even though she didn't know how things were going to turn out, she followed Him. Today, her daughter is alive with a loving family. And Jane is with Jesus for all eternity.

Are you willing to take up your cross daily and follow Him *wherever He leads?*

HIS WORD
"Whoever wants to save his life will lose it, but whoever loses his life for me will save it" (Luke 9:24).

MY PART
Many times throughout our lifetime, we are faced with difficult decisions. But we have a guidebook and a Counselor to help us. When we follow God's commands, we will always come out better. Next time you have a big decision, seek instruction through His Word and prayer.

MY STUDY
Proverbs 7:1–3; Isaiah 25:8

We women often spend a lot of time on our appearance. There's nothing inherently wrong with that or with wanting to represent God well. Appearances do make a difference! But the beauty that God cares more about is on the inside.

Unfading Beauty

Besides the many general principles in the Bible that can be applied to both men and women, Proverbs 31 speaks specifically to us women. It describes the kind of woman we should all strive to be:

> She is worth far more than rubies. Her husband has full confidence in her…She sets about her work vigorously …She opens her arms to the poor…is clothed with strength and dignity…speaks with wisdom, and faithful instruction is on her tongue. She watches over the affairs of her household.

Wow! That's quite a list—and there's more to it. Don't be discouraged, friend. God doesn't expect you to fulfill perfectly every single item on that list. It is meant to be a goal to which all women can strive. If you rely on God for guidance in your daily decisions, you will find that many of these items will become less difficult.

Proverbs 31 ends like this: "Charm is deceptive, and beauty is fleeting; but a woman who fears the LORD is to be praised...Let her works bring her praise" (v. 31). External appearances don't tell the whole truth about someone, and they will fade with time. The qualities that will be praised by God and people are those that come from an intimate, daily walk with Him. Through the Holy Spirit, God will produce in us what we read in Proverbs 31.

Friend, cultivate your relationship with God. Spend time reading His Word and talking with Him. Under His power, seek to exhibit the characteristics of a "Proverbs 31" woman—wisdom, compassion, dignity, and reliability. Then when your outer beauty fades, it won't matter—to you or anyone else.

HIS WORD

"Who is wise and understanding among you? Let him show it by his good life, by deeds done in the humility that comes from wisdom" *(James 3:13).*

MY PART

Read all of Proverbs 31. Think in practical terms about how these qualities can fit into your life. How can you cultivate them to become more like the Proverbs 31 woman? Remember, this is not something you achieve under your own power but through God's power.

MY STUDY

Job 28:28; Psalm 111:10

DAY 57

If you had seven days left to live, what would you do with them?

Ramona was asked this question, and it forced her to reevaluate her life. She asked herself: *What would I do first? Straighten out my finances? Organize my desk and photo albums? Or make the most of time with friends and loved ones?*

Priorities

None of us knows the time at which we will leave this earth. God alone has power over life and death. Even so, it is useful to keep our mortality in focus. Thinking about how short life really is forces us to think about our true priorities.

Contemplating this question, Ramona concluded what her true priorities are. The first was her relationship with Christ. As with close human relationships, it is important to work at maintaining our intimacy with Christ. We maintain closeness through conversation (prayer) and understanding (studying the Bible).

Next, Ramona discovered that serving others was very important. Even though Jesus was God, He demonstrated servanthood when He washed the disciples' feet.

They were stunned by this supreme act of humility. In John 13:15 Jesus puts His act in perspective for them. He says, "I have set you an example that you should do as I have done for you." When we serve others we are doing as Jesus would want us to do.

Last, Ramona realized the great value of setting aside times for refreshing. She said, "It's so easy to get caught up in day-to-day duties and miss the joy and true meaning of life."

When we slow down to reconnect with God, we are better able to see the beauty around us. We are better able to hear the still small voice inside us, which is the Holy Spirit guiding and directing.

Friend, you can reset your priorities today. What is truly important to you? Think about it.

HIS WORD

"Teach us to number our days aright, that we may gain a heart of wisdom" (Psalm 90:12).

MY PART

"Father, am I spending my time to the greatest advantage? Show me what's most important to You. I ask Your guidance to help me rearrange my schedule today to reflect Your will and my true priorities. Remind me to do this every day, to live a life sold out to You, a life that will bring the greatest satisfaction, peace, and joy."

MY STUDY
Ecclesiastes 8:5,6; Romans 13:11–14

DAY 58

Thomas Traore is a pastor in West Africa. A passion for evangelism was born in Pastor Traore at *Amsterdam* '86, an international conference sponsored by the Billy Graham Evangelistic Association. What he learned changed his heart, then his church.

Sharing Life

Pastor Traore said, "My church has made evangelism its highest priority. When a new Christian joins the church, the first thing we try to teach him is that he is an evangelist, too; that he too should go out and witness and lead people to God."

Becoming a Christian changes your life—for all eternity. What more loving thing could you do for a fellow human being than to introduce that person to the Source of true life?

Not only is it the loving thing do to, God expects us to do it—He commands us to do it. It is called the Great Commission. In Matthew 28:18,19, Jesus said, "All authority in heaven and on earth has been given to me. Therefore go and make disciples of all nations, baptizing them in the name of the Father and of the Son and of the Holy Spirit." So Jesus, as the ultimate authority, has given us a directive.

As we go about our daily lives, we are to keep constantly in our minds the fact that many around us are not yet disciples (followers) of Christ, and will spend eternity away from God. This should motivate us to seek out ways to share the gospel with those we encounter. Don't be intimidated; just share what Christ has done for you and how they can share in this eternal life.

Today, make a list of friends and neighbors who need to know God. Then make it a priority to tell them about God's redeeming love. You can use the information in the back of this book to assist you. You too can help change the world!

HIS WORD

"I will extol the LORD at all times; his praise will always be on my lips" (Psalm 34:1).

MY PART

"Lord Jesus, my Savior, thank You for Your gift of salvation. I want to help others come to know You. Help me to be sensitive to Your leading, that I may be bold and courageous as I tell them of Your love. In Your holy name, amen."

MY STUDY

1 Chronicles 16:23–25; 2 Peter 3:8,9

Twenty-year-old John Bisagno was engaged to be married, finishing college, and going into the ministry. His future father-in-law, Dr. Paul Beck, shared a bit of advice with John to prepare him for the challenges he'd surely face.

Stay True to Jesus

A minister for many years, Dr. Beck had observed many young people going into vocational service for God. His simple yet profound words were, "John, stay true to Jesus! Make sure you keep your heart close to Jesus every day."

Dr. Beck found that just one in ten people who began full-time service for the Lord at age twenty-one had stayed on track until age sixty-five. Discouragement, moral failure, financial pressures, and other issues robbed them of the joy of ministry.

Shocked and incredulous, John went home and wrote in his Bible the names of twenty-four men who were his peers. Christians, walking with God, they all shared a common desire to be used by God and were trained in ministry.

John served as pastor of the First Baptist Church of

Houston for many years. He stayed true to Jesus. Sadly, from time to time, he's had to turn to that page in his Bible and mark out another name. After thirty-three years, only three of those twenty-four men had stayed true to Jesus.

Author and speaker Steve Farrar told John's story in his book *Finishing Strong*. Steve wrote these words, "In the Christian life, it's not how you start that matters. It's how you finish."

Finishing strong, dear friend, means staying true to Jesus. It applies to us all. No matter who you are or what your occupation, staying true to Jesus all your life is what matters most. It means walking with Him moment by moment, every day. You do that by spending time with Him—reading His Word and talking to Him in prayer.

Stay true to Jesus. He always stays true to you. He sets you free and enables you to finish strong.

HIS WORD
"When he arrived and saw the evidence of the grace of God, he was glad and encouraged them all to remain true to the Lord with all their hearts" (Acts 11:23).

MY PART
Maybe today, you've already lost your way. Perhaps you're discouraged, or you've failed morally. You feel stuck. Dear friend, tell God right now about those defeats. Talk to Him. Entrust your heart into His hands. It's never to late to find forgiveness and start your healing!

MY STUDY
Jeremiah 23:24; Psalm 64:10

Cynthia will never forget a special time with her father when she was twelve years old. They'd planned it for months! *Finally*, the big day had arrived. Their night on the town was to include Chinatown, a movie, cable cars, and hot fudge sundaes.

Let Your "Yes" Be "Yes"

So she traveled with her dad on a business trip to San Francisco. After his meetings, her dad returned to the hotel. But with him was an influential client, who invited them to dinner.

Cynthia held her breath. Would her father choose the client over her? Would all their plans be ruined? Cynthia sighed with relief when her father politely declined. He explained he'd planned a special evening with his daughter. Cynthia loved her dad for keeping his promise!

Her dad understood the importance of keeping his word, especially to his daughter. In Matthew 5:33 we're told, "Do not break your oath...Simply let your 'Yes' be 'Yes,' and your 'No,' 'No.'" It's as simple as that.

Keeping your word is one of the most obvious indicators of the kind of character you have. It is particularly important to your children. Not only do they observe how you keep your word with others, but they also have good memories. And they trust you. When you don't keep your promises to them, they will remember, and your failure will chip away at their implicit trust.

Dear friend, I know sometimes it is difficult, but to the best of your ability, keep your promises to your children. By doing so, you are demonstrating to them that at least one of the two adults they count on most in the world is worthy of their trust. It will give them a security that is invaluable. That kind of atmosphere will help them grow and you will develop a closer relationship with them. And in you, it will build an honorable character!

HIS WORD
"Sons are a heritage from the LORD, children a reward from him" (Psalm 127:3).

MY PART
"Father of all truth, thank You for keeping all of Your promises. It is an example I want to follow in my own life, with those around me. May I always keep my promises, especially to my children. In Jesus' name, amen."

MY STUDY
Deuteronomy 6:6–8; Mark 10:14

The Caring Heart

He who refreshes others will himself
be refreshed.

PROVERBS 11:25

Being alone is more than a physical reality. A recent study, in which 66 percent of respondents said they were lonely, concluded that this is one of the greatest changes in women's lives. With over half of adult women working outside the home and living in heavily populated urban areas, loneliness seems impossible.

Unlike our mothers who often lived their entire lives in the same town with relatives, we are very mobile. But this mobility leaves us little opportunity to develop relationships that nurture our emotional and spiritual needs.

Every believer has the Holy Spirit as a source of comfort and strength, and complete satisfaction can be found only in a relationship with Jesus. But we also need relationships with others.

Think about your relationships in three categories:

- *Casual:* Acquaintances—You meet these people in social settings on an irregular basis. These are people with whom you can share your faith.
- *Close:* Friends—You see these people on a regular basis, and have the privilege of forming close, personal friendships.
- *Covenant:* Family—Your family members are precious gifts from God and deserve your commitment to their development. Spend time with them and guard them from ungodly influences. Remember: you choose your friends, God chose your family.

When Bill and I were newly married, we left our home state of Oklahoma for California. Only a few short weeks after unpacking, we entertained in our new home. Bill had met a businessman who didn't know Christ and invited him and his wife to dinner.

The Contract

I had much to learn about what God expected for hospitality. The only dishes I had to complete four settings were green glass "oatmeal china." I was elated that my dinner was scheduled on St. Patrick's Day. How appropriate that we had green "china."

We spent the evening sharing our faith with the businessman and his wife. At that time, Bill and I were very inexperienced in how to lead a person to Christ, but the couple was responsive to what we said. I began to understand how to use what we had to bring honor and glory to Christ, and this began an exciting lifelong journey of ministry with Him.

The Lord was preparing our hearts for our second year of marriage, when Bill suggested that we sign a contract with God, totally surrendering our lives to Him. Bill had signed hundreds of contracts as a businessman, so an agreement between the Lord and us seemed reasonable to him.

That contract has formed the basis of our lives and ministry. We surrendered our lives completely and irrevocably to the Lord and to each other. Sharing our faith immediately became a lifestyle.

God is gracious! He places no value on our possessions. He doesn't pressure us to perform, or require us to be sophisticated. Instead, He sees our hearts and understands our needs. Through the power of His Holy Spirit, He uses us where we live to help heal the hurts and broken spirits of those who need His love. Relying on His strength and wisdom, I learned confidence in life sharing.

Have you given everything you are and have to God? That's the greatest decision you can make as a believer. It will set your life on a course far different and more glorious than you ever dreamed.

HIS WORD
"Here is a trustworthy saying: If we died with him, we shall also live with him; if we endure, we shall also reign with him" *(2 Timothy 2:11,12).*

MY PART
Our lives are more than a chronology of events. Turn your life over to God's complete control. Reaffirm your decision daily as you walk with Him.

MY STUDY
Exodus 32:29; Psalm 16:7,8

Few of us would argue that women tend to be more relational than men. But for busy women these days, sometimes valuable time with friends gets squeezed out.

Do you have a *soul mate?* Is there someone in your life with whom you can share your deepest feelings, fears, and frustrations?

Soul Mates

I have heard this description of a best friend. Maybe you'll identify with this:

"There's very little we can't say to each other. Our relationship is based on a sense of trust and years of maturing together. We share the good and the bad. We play together and pray together. And in emotional emergencies, we're there for each other."

Do you have a friend like that?

The Bible contains many examples of this kind of friendship: Elizabeth and Mary, Ruth and Naomi, David and Jonathan. Each of these pairs not only acted as confidantes, but also as spiritual guides and supporters.

I think friendship with other women is more necessary today than ever before. But it can also be more difficult.

In this journey of life, we're called to a variety of responsibilities. For some, this entails being the wife of a husband, the mother of children, or the keeper of a home. For others, it is a call to singleness, a life spent in service to God and to others. To make an impact for Christ, we must work together.

Someone has said that to have friends you have to make yourself friendly. I encourage you to take the next step toward developing a close relationship with at least one other woman.

As with any worthwhile effort, building deep friendships takes an investment of time and a sacrifice of personal desires. The foundation should be spiritual to give an eternal perspective. And the relationship should involve lighthearted fun. A true friend nurtures your soul, as you nurture theirs.

HIS WORD
"Two are better than one, because they have a good return for their work. If one falls down, his friend can help him up" *(Ecclesiastes 4:9,10).*

MY PART
Seek to become acquainted with someone you would like to get to know better. Develop a relationship that includes prayer and Bible study and times just to catch up and share what's on your heart. Schedule regular visits with your friends. God often uses the platform of friendship to foster spiritual growth and maturity.

MY STUDY
Proverbs 27:10
Romans 16:3,4

A friend of mine has six children, including two high schoolers, living at home. At times she has felt overwhelmed, as if her parenting responsibilities were about to crash in around her.

Encouraging Others

In the middle of this difficult and busy time, some younger mothers approached her, asking if she would meet with them once a month. They wanted encouragement and advice about parenting. My friend thought, *Why would they want to come to meet with me, after all the mistakes I've made? What do I have to offer them?*

However, she knew what Titus 2 says about older, godly women influencing younger women, because as a young mother she had been mentored by an older woman. Young women need mentoring and encouragement from more mature women who have walked the same path, even if they too have stumbled a few times along the way.

You may have to do a little prayerful searching for a

mentor. Ask God to help you spot someone who's just ahead of your season in life and can counsel you from her experience. Your church family is the best place to start. The main point is to find someone who has established a track record of walking with God.

Take the initiative to ask if you can phone her or meet her for coffee or lunch. Tell her you'll bring the questions—all she needs to do is listen and share with you. Assure her she doesn't even need to know all the answers; all you need is her time and perspective.

If someone happens to ask *you* to take on the role of mentor, don't resist the opportunity. Wives and mothers don't need help from a Superwoman—they need a friend who has walked some distance in their shoes. I'll always be grateful for those women who helped me in my early years as a wife and mother.

HIS WORD

"Apply your heart to instruction and your ears to words of knowledge" (Proverbs 32:12).

MY PART

Mentoring doesn't have to be a formal meeting or arrangement. It can be a lifestyle situation. It's as simple as spending time with someone you're committed to praying for and encouraging. Keep your eyes open to these rewarding opportunities.

MY STUDY

Ecclesiastes 12:9,10; Titus 2:3–5

Guilty *as charged!*" Only Lois and Steve can fully identify with the shock of hearing those words in a court of law.

Lois and Steve are Christians, and quite active in their local church. Through a very strange and complex sequence of events, Steve was falsely accused and convicted of murder. He was sentenced to forty years in a maximum-security prison.

Our Advocate

We can only imagine the devastation that must have struck their family—not only Lois and their three young children, but the extended family as well.

Lois would not be shaken. Never doubting his innocence for a moment, she stood by her husband throughout the entire ordeal. With three precious children and her whole life ahead, Lois could have left Steve to start over, but she chose to honor the vows of her marriage.

She persisted in her fight to convince authorities that Steve was not guilty as charged. Finally, in a subsequent court case, the truth was exposed. The investigating officers had fabricated their evidence to obtain a quick conviction.

Steve was immediately released from prison to resume his life—after three-and-a-half years behind bars. Today, Steve says that Lois was his life support while he endured the nightmare.

In much the same way, every one of us has been given a life sentence. But, unlike Steve, we are guilty. The charge, of course, is sin. The sentence is an eternity in hell, separated from God and our loved ones.

When the gavel of divine justice slams down in God's courtroom, and the word "guilty" defines our status, that's when Jesus steps forward as our Advocate. He paid the penalty for our sin by dying on our behalf.

It is my hope and prayer today that you will acknowledge His love for you. Although you have been found guilty of sin, He stands by your side, waiting for you to respond to His love and forgiveness.

HIS WORD

"Be imitators of God, therefore, as dearly loved children and live a life of love, just as Christ loved us and gave himself up for us as a fragrant offering and sacrifice to God" *(Ephesians 5:1,2).*

MY PART

Guilty as charged! Those three words impacted Steve and Lois forever. But in God's courtroom, another word applies: forgiven! If you've never experienced God's complete forgiveness, turn to the back of this book and find out how.

MY STUDY

Nehemiah 9:26,27; Psalm 51:1,2

We've all seen them. Leaning against buildings, waiting by the curb, dressed provocatively—some pitifully young. We often respond with judgment. Or sarcasm. Or even disdain.

Remember when Jesus encountered the prostitute in Simon's home (Luke 7:36–50)? Simon was a prominent Pharisee in the first century.

Loving the Unlovely

It was customary for dinner guests to recline around a low table, propped up on their elbows to eat the meal. In this setting, they would often discuss politics and religion. Uninvited neighbors were free to come and listen to the discussions without partaking of the meal.

While the others in the room listened to the conversation, the sinful woman was on a different mission. She had heard about Jesus, and she came to bring him an expensive gift—precious perfume in an alabaster jar.

The Bible tells us that she approached the table behind Jesus, clutching the gift in her hands. She began to weep, and her tears splashed on Jesus' feet. Spontaneously showing her reverence and affection, she attempted to dry His feet with her hair. She kissed His feet, in an act of love and respect, and poured the precious perfume on them.

Can you picture the response? The room became very quiet. Simon was disgusted. The guests were shocked because they knew this woman's reputation. But when Simon grew indignant, Jesus rebuked him.

Jesus responded to the woman's expression of love by saying, "Your sins are forgiven. Your faith has saved you; go in peace."

The woman had given Jesus love. Jesus had given her peace. To Him, she was His priceless creation, made in God's image.

Dear friend, the next time you are in the presence of someone you find unlovely, remember the behavior that Jesus modeled for you.

HIS WORD
"This is my prayer: that your love may abound more and more in knowledge and depth of insight" (Philippians 1:9).

MY PART
"Loving Lord Jesus, Your beautiful example of love and forgiveness is one I want to follow in my life. I want Your indwelling Spirit to guide me daily so I may speak Your love to hurting hearts. In Your precious name, amen."

MY STUDY
Ruth 2:8–13; Psalm 133:1–3

Cartoon heroes are easy to spot. They have flashy costumes, muscles of steel, and booming voices to make their presence known.

Real life heroes are a bit different. They look like you and me. They get tired, even sick at times. They probably don't recognize themselves as heroes. In fact, it may never even occur to them.

Somebody's Hero

Millions of men, women, and children lost their lives during the holocaust. Throughout this ugly era of world history, many heroes valiantly attempted to rescue the men and women under persecution.

As a young woman, Stephanie hid thirteen Jews in her tiny apartment attic for two years. Her family knew nothing of this, and had she been discovered, it would have cost Stephanie her life.

We all know the heroic acts of Corrie ten Boom who spent years in a concentration camp after she was caught protecting the lives of others.

Who has marked your life in a significant way? Who is your hero?

I immediately think of my mother, Margaret Zachary, a model of stability, commitment, and faith. I also thank God for Henrietta Mears who inspired both Bill and me to be involved in full-time Christian work.

Have you stopped to realize that you could be someone's hero? Someone in your sphere of influence takes his or her cues from your example. Are you living up to that expectation?

You may never need to risk your life to hide someone in your attic, but you can be sure there are those who look to you as a model of character, integrity, Christian conviction, and faith.

Nothing will make a greater impact on America and the world than women who are sold out to Jesus Christ—leading holy lives of faith, walking daily in the power of the Holy Spirit, and sharing their faith. They are the true heroes of our generation.

HIS WORD
"He has given us this command: Whoever loves God must also love his brother" (1 John 4:21).

MY PART
You may not feel like a hero today, my dear friend, but take another look at that toddler around your knees. Some of the greatest men and women in leadership in this generation pay honor to their mothers as heroes in their lives. You have an important role in your children's lives, as well as in the lives of those around you.

MY STUDY
Proverbs 17:17; Job 29:15,16

Every day, men and women leave their native land to live in the United States. They come in pursuit of the American dream.

This migration brings a world of opportunity to our doorstep.

A Melting Pot

Still, there are sensitive cultural and economic implications when minorities flood a society. Since God has allowed this wide breadth of cultures to join our own, we have the wonderful opportunity of welcoming many of them as brothers and sisters in Christ. We can expose others to biblical truth and share our Christian heritage as never before.

The vast array of cultures in the U.S. also means we find the influence of world religions right next door—Muslims, Hindus, and Buddhists, just to name a few.

I'm afraid that many Christians withdraw from these people. Instead of accepting their cultural influences as a wonderful opportunity, some American believers choose to be isolated, rather than visionary; intolerant, rather than loving.

Wouldn't it be much better if immigrants discovered

what made our country so great? Newcomers should be enlightened about our rich Christian heritage and those who founded this nation on biblical principles.

Think about your own neighborhood, your own town. Have you seen the influx of different races and religions? Do their lifestyles irritate you or are you extending God's love to them?

How about going to the home of those new neighbors and welcoming them to the community? Let them know you're glad they're on your street. Build a relationship with them that creates an atmosphere of trust and respect.

Don't hesitate to ask them questions about their cultural traditions. Become a student of their heritage. When you take the time, you will find that right next door is a world of opportunity—opportunity to share the gospel.

HIS WORD
"You will receive power when the Holy Spirit comes on you; and you will be my witnesses in Jerusalem, and in all Judea and Samaria, and to the ends of the earth" (Acts 1:8).

MY PART
Pray for opportunities to share your faith and ask God to give you a spirit of understanding. He will help you know what to say and when to say it. Immigrants you befriend may ask you questions, wanting to know more about your faith. You can tell them about Jesus and what He's done for you.

MY STUDY
Leviticus 19:34; Psalm 146:9

The United States is the most mobile society in the world. No other nation moves from home to home, city to city, or state to state as frequently as we do.

If you live in a neighborhood with a lot of turnover, it may not be unusual for you to see a new family move in and then realize that you didn't take the time to get acquainted with the family that moved out!

People on the Move

After that happened to some friends of ours, they determined not to let it happen again. So when the house across the street had a "Sold" sign on it, they began preparing and praying for their new neighbors. On move-in day, they immediately crossed the street and introduced themselves and their children.

For the next week, they offered to help the newcomers get situated in their new home, providing whatever they could to make it easier—tools, ice, even meals. They gave input about the nearest hardware store, the best grocery store, and the local schools.

Then they introduced the two young children to playmates in the neighborhood.

Finally, they planned a weekend block party for all the neighbors in the cul-de-sac, a time for everyone to get acquainted. The invitation included a map of all the homes on the street with the names of the people who lived in each house.

The barbecue and block party brought all the friends and neighbors together. It provided a wonderful starting point for relationships that continue.

The journey of a lasting friendship starts with one step—a step toward your neighbor's door. This may seem like a small step, but it is much more than that! Dear friend, don't miss out on an opportunity to shine the light of Christ in your neighborhood.

HIS WORD
"Do not withhold good from those who deserve it, when it is in your power to act. Do not say to your neighbor, 'Come back later; I'll give it tomorrow'—when you now have it with you" (Proverbs 3:27,28).

MY PART
"Oh, Father, I confess sometimes it's easier to keep to myself than to break the ice and make new friends. But I cannot keep the message of hope to myself! Lord, show me how to reach out to my neighbors, letting them know that I care and that You care about them."

MY STUDY
Deuteronomy 10:17–19; 1 John 4:7–12

've never known anyone who lives what they believe like you do." Dianne's supervisor said those words to her on her last day on the job. That led Dianne to reflect on the lessons God taught her at work.

She learned to pray. As a new Christian, she felt inadequate to share her faith. So she prayed for her coworkers daily as she drove to work. She always asked God to give her the opportunity to share about Him.

Office Encounters

She also began to speak openly about church activities and Bible studies, and to bring a Christian perspective to office conversations, especially those involving major news stories or local tragedies.

She allowed others to glimpse her life before Christ. When appropriate, she'd tell a story from her former life so others could see God's changing power.

Seeing coworkers through Jesus' eyes was an invaluable lesson. When tempted to avoid someone who irritated her, she made an effort to view that person as someone Jesus loves.

Finally, she learned to not be surprised by rejection. Dianne didn't let those who rejected her message keep her from gently sharing Christ with others who might be more responsive.

On her last day at work, Dianne gave each coworker a book or CD that would point them to Christ. She included a personal note telling them about God's love. She was determined to leave something in their hands that contained the gospel.

In their closing conversation, Dianne's supervisor asked how she became a Christian. For the first time, Dianne gave her full testimony to her supervisor.

Dear friend, what a beautiful example Diane is of a Christian devoted to living a life for the glory of God and His kingdom. Perhaps you too can use in your life the lessons Dianne has learned.

HIS WORD

"'You are my witnesses,' declares the LORD, 'and my servants whom I have chosen!'" (Isaiah 43:10).

MY PART

God will give you opportunities to share. Just ask Him. Pray for the courage to speak up, and pray for each of your coworkers. You don't have to know everything about their lives or how they will respond. God uses willing hearts. He'll use you if you let Him!

MY STUDY

Proverbs 31:26; Matthew 25:34–40

I'd like to share with you one of the most heartwarming love stories I've ever heard.

Dr. Ed Wheat, a popular Christian psychologist, wrote this touching account in his book *Love Life for Every Married Couple*.

Unconditional Love

A man loved his wife tenderly and steadfastly for fifteen years without any reciprocal love on her part. There could be no response because she had developed a brain disease.

At the onset of the disease, she was a pretty, vivacious lady of sixty who looked at least ten years younger. Initially, she experienced intermittent times of confusion. As the disease progressed, she gradually lost all her mental faculties and did not recognize her husband.

For the first five years, he took care of her at home by himself. During that time, he often took her for visits. Although she had no idea where she was, she looked her prettiest, and he proudly displayed her as his wife.

He never made an apology for her; he never indicated that there was anything wrong with what she said.

The time came when the doctors said she had to go into a nursing home for intensive care. She lived in the home for ten years—and he was with her daily, never in any way embarrassed that she was so far out of touch.

This was unconditional love, not in theory, but in practice!

Dr. Wheat concludes the story with this statement: "I can speak of this case with intimate knowledge, for these people were my own wonderful parents."

Are you trying to change someone to make him or her more lovable? The solution lies not in changing your loved one, but in changing the way you love! You must learn to love by Christ's example—unconditionally.

HIS WORD

"My command is this: Love each other as I have loved you. Greater love has no one than this, that he lay down his life for his friends" (John 15:12,13).

MY PART

Become a reflection of God's love in your home, at your work, in your neighborhood, and in your community. When you choose to love unconditionally, you will become a model of God's love to a dying world.

MY STUDY

Proverbs 9:9; Isaiah 63:7

It wasn't a huge argument, just silly, angry words. But it hurt. Her husband's last remark before he left for work prompted something ugly inside her to retaliate, insult for insult. She couldn't erase the incident or her anger from her mind.

The Chalkboard Lesson

Later, her son sat on the kitchen floor, writing on something. The sound of the soft scratching floated in the air: *Scribble. Scribble . . . swish.* Sue stepped around him, busy with dinner and nursing her grudge. She found her attention focusing on the peculiar pattern of sound her son made: *Scribble. Scribble . . . swish.* Finally, Sue paused and looked down at him.

Her son's hand clutched a stubby piece of chalk as he scribbled on a slate. Then in one quick movement, he swished the eraser across it. The scribble marks disappeared.

Sue discovered a hidden lesson. Husbands and wives are human. They have moments of failure, scribbling on one another's lives, leaving dark, ugly words—ones that mar and wound. The work of forgiveness makes the scribble vanish, erases the wrong, and remembers it no more.

"Lord," Sue prayed right then, "I've been so wrong to cling to this small, scribbled slate of wrong done to me. With Your help, I erase it now, wiping away every mark placed there. It's forgiven." *Swish*. The sound of forgiveness seemed to echo in her heart. And it was done without a moment to spare. Just home from work, Sue's husband breezed through the door. His look was more uncertain than angry. "About this morning," he began, looking at the floor and then at her. "I'm sor…"

"Oh, I'm sorry too!" she exclaimed without hesitation. As they embraced in the kitchen, all was silent except for a faint and magical swish somewhere in the room.

HIS WORD

"Bear with each other and forgive whatever grievances you may have against one another. Forgive as the Lord forgave you. And over all these virtues put on love, which binds them all together in perfect unity" (Colossians 3:13,14).

MY PART

Forgiveness is not optional, no matter how large or small the offense. Christ has forgiven us, so we must also forgive others. Using your Bible concordance, look up all the references on forgiveness. God has the power to forgive. His power is there for you. By His Spirit, you can forgive others.

MY STUDY

Genesis 45:1–15; Proverbs 27:9

A friend of mine was going through a rough time after moving to a new place. She expected it to take a while to make some new friends—but not *two years!*

Surrounded by people every day at work, she still felt lonely and isolated.

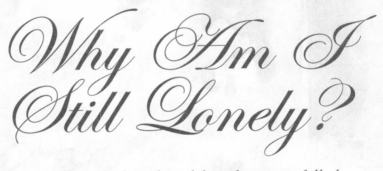

Why Am I Still Lonely?

I was proud of my friend for asking painfully honest questions. She wondered, *If God is such a great companion, why do I still feel so lonely?* I'm glad to say that her honesty led to a discovery.

At first, she concluded it was a spiritual problem. So she began to spend more time with God in prayer. Finally, she realized it was people—God's people—she needed.

As Christians, we really do need each other! Consider Adam. Isn't it interesting that Adam had it all—including a perfect relationship with God—and still, he had a need for companionship? God provided Eve, his helper.

God made each of us with a need to connect—a need to have a relationship, first with Him and then with other people.

Christ is all-sufficient and meets all of our needs in many different ways. One of His favorite tools is another believer—someone to distribute love and grace.

You may live in the most populated area in the country, surrounded by people. Yet there's an emptiness in your life.

Don't immediately assume that there's something wrong in your relationship with God. He created you to need people in your life.

Let me encourage you to take the initiative. *Be* a friend. Connect with another person. Even if you're not feeling friendly right now, someone around you is. Take time to ask that person questions. Your interest will not only help your friend, but will also alleviate your loneliness.

The scriptural principal works!

HIS WORD

"Be devoted to one another in brotherly love. Honor one another above yourselves" (Romans 12:10).

MY PART

Learn how to love. Loving others, as an expression of your faith, is often the greatest cure for feeling lonely. First, seek out new people to get to know. Then, start talking to them; find out about their lives; and tell them about yours. Before you know it, you will have a new connection.

MY STUDY

1 Samuel 18:1–4; Proverbs 10:12

Some call *listening* the work of genuine love.

Have you ever thought about how others perceive your ability to listen? You may be listening to every word, but if the person speaking doesn't know you are listening, they may feel ignored or even rejected.

Are You Listening?

A friend tells about a little boy in her Sunday school who held onto her leg and chattered away while she was trying to greet parents and students at the classroom door. Finally, in total exasperation, he raised his voice and said, "Teacher, you are not listening to me!"

The teacher stooped down to him and said, "Yes, I am listening."

The little boy responded, "Not with your eyes."

Someone observed that God created us with two ears and one mouth so we should listen twice as much as we talk. Maybe we should also remember that we have two eyes. Those eyes making contact with someone can establish the fact that we are indeed listening.

Listening involves more than just hearing the words spoken. Think about listening to a hymn or praise song. Really hearing the lyrics impacts our emotions and evokes an attitude of worship. In the same way, really listening to someone communicates respect. We signal that we are taking in everything they are saying and are giving them our undivided attention.

The following items show the importance of listening:

- The Bible says listening to God and wise counselors shows true wisdom.
- Surveys show children who listen well do better in school.
- Listening enhances relationships and increases success.
- The Book of Proverbs is full of admonitions to "listen," "hearken," "hear," "attend," and "give ear to."

Be a good listener. It takes work but shows genuine love and true biblical wisdom.

HIS WORD

"Let the wise listen and add to their learning, and let the discerning get guidance" (Proverbs 1:5).

MY PART

Ask God to help you be a good listener. You can practice listening. First, stop what you're doing. Second, focus your undivided attention by looking the other person in the eyes. Third, ask a question to clarify. Fourth, rephrase what you've heard. That shows you've listened.

MY STUDY

Ecclesiastes 9:16; Mark 9:7,8

One of my favorite women in the Bible is Ruth. She was an incredible lady and a committed friend.

The main character in the Book of Ruth is Naomi. Naomi, her husband, and her two sons moved to another country to escape a severe famine. Over the next ten years, Naomi's two sons married foreign women, Orpah and Ruth.

'Til Death Do Us Part

All was going well until tragedy struck. Naomi's husband died, as well as their two sons.

As a widow with no one to support her, Naomi decided to return to her hometown. She didn't expect her two daughters-in-law to go with her. They would be foreigners, and she could promise them only a life of poverty and prejudice.

That's when Ruth made her incredible statement:

Don't urge me to leave you or to turn back from you. Where you go I will go, and where you stay I will stay. Your people will be my people and your God my God.

Where you die I will die, and there I will be buried. May the Lord deal with me, be it ever so severely, if anything but death separates you and me (Ruth 1:16,17).

What a friend! Consider five very quick lessons about the benefits of committed relationships.

First, committed friends enable us to give and receive love.

Second, committed relationships foster a secure identity. Ruth and Naomi enjoyed a sense of belonging to each other.

Third, committed relationships provide physical protection and material needs.

Fourth, committed relationships have the potential of providing the deepest fulfillment of which we're capable. This happens when each person wants to do what is best for the other.

Committed relationships help us grasp God's commitment to us.

HIS WORD
"A friend loves at all times, and a brother is born for adversity" *(Proverbs 17:17).*

MY PART
"Loving heavenly Father, thank You for Your unconditional love, even with all of my imperfections. Help me to show Your love to those around me. Help me to be a good friend to those closest to me. I want to be a walking example of Your infinite love to the world. Amen."

MY STUDY
Malachi 3:16; Acts 2:46,47

When Barry and Nancy married, they weren't believers. But Nancy's coworkers were, and they lived a beautiful Christian example before her and answered her many questions. Then one day Nancy simply prayed, "Jesus save me."

Twenty-one Years of Prayer

That prayer changed her life and launched Nancy into a new adventure. Unfortunately, the excitement of the spiritual adventure for Nancy caused her marriage to suffer. For the first year, she lived out a daily campaign to push her faith on Barry. She preached and left open Bibles around the house.

Nancy's behavior was destroying her marriage. Barry wanted his "old" wife back.

A Christian coworker gave Nancy a book about prayer. That book opened Nancy's eyes to what her responsibility was toward her husband. She simply had to trust God to reach Barry's heart. She read and reread the book, putting into practice what she learned. She prayed for Barry, loved him, and was available to discuss spiritual matters. She was careful to let Barry initiate the questions and did not try to go beyond his interest level. Nancy accepted the fact that only the Holy Spirit could convict Barry and bring him to a point of accepting Christ. Her responsibility was to live a godly life and love Barry as her husband.

After twenty-one years, she's still loving Barry and praying he'll someday trust Christ.

It's so difficult to understand how a mate could resist the desire to accept Christ as Savior when an example of His love and grace is being lived out in the home every day. I certainly don't know how to explain it. But I do know that many, many times an unbeliever accepts Christ as a result of the influence of his spouse. No matter what the situation, trusting God is the only option. He alone can change a heart.

HIS WORD
"Be strong in the Lord and in his mighty power" (Ephesians 6:10).

MY PART
Are there people close to you who don't know Christ? Perhaps a spouse, a parent, a brother or sister, or maybe a friend. The best thing you can do for them is to love them with the love Christ has given you, pray for them, and be ready —when the time comes—to share Christ with them.

MY STUDY
Proverbs 18:10; Isaiah 8:17

Melissa was judgmental, constantly belittling Suzy's faith. Melissa and Suzy had been neighbors for years, and their children spent a lot of time playing together. The children frequently would repeat a comment that Melissa had made about Suzy's beliefs. Suzy's heart would ache. The children didn't understand the deep meaning of what was going on, and Melissa's children were nice friends.

Living Your Christian Faith

Many nights Suzy would pray, "God, bring someone else to minister to her!" But the Lord always responded that He could help her love Melissa. She knew that if they had a major philosophical disagreement or an open debate about religion, it would have made things worse.

Suzy knew that she must live a consistent and faithful life before Melissa. When the family drove off for church on Sunday, Suzy would always wave or shout out the window, "Have a nice day."

Suzy realized that if she couldn't win Melissa, at least she could share her faith with the children. Melissa did allow her children to go to Vacation Bible School with Suzy's children, and they had a great time. One of them accepted Christ as Savior and began attending church regularly.

When a "For Sale" sign went up in Melissa's yard, Suzy was surprised. The house sold quickly, and Suzy offered to help Melissa pack. As they packed things for the movers, Suzy picked up an old family Bible. Melissa explained that it had belonged to her grandmother. Suzy told Melissa that no matter where she lived, if she ever wanted to talk about spiritual things, Suzy would be available.

Melissa's reply was encouraging: "Suzy, I've watched you, and you really live your Christian faith. I'm beginning to think more about it."

A life led in obedience to Christ is the best witness you can give of Christ's love.

HIS WORD
"You yourselves are our letter, written on our hearts, known and read by everybody" (2 Corinthians 3:2).

MY PART
"Dear Father, sometimes a daily witness is more difficult than just telling someone what it means to be a Christian. Please, dear Father, let my life reflect the love of Jesus enough to penetrate the heart of even a difficult person. I ask Your help to keep my attitudes what they should be to honor You. In Jesus' holy name, amen."

MY STUDY
2 Chronicles 31:20,21; Psalm 34:11,12

The first time I received a letter from Linda, she asked for my suggestions on helping high-school students improve the moral fiber of their community. She was a teacher who worked closely with teenagers. After that, Linda wrote regularly to tell me about her work and the exciting opportunities she had to see many students come to know Christ.

Beyond Appearances

I heard from Linda for three years, then learned she had volunteered to care for the children during a Campus Crusade Staff Training. I eagerly anticipated meeting her. After talking with Linda and arranging a time for us to meet, a friend said, "Linda doesn't think you'll like her after you see her." I realized from her comment that Linda had a physical handicap or deformity.

Later that week we were introduced. As she talked, she anchored her elbow in one hand to hold her chin steady as she tried to speak coherently. It was a joyful experience for both of us as we talked briefly. As she turned to leave, I recognized the spastic condition of her frail body. Seldom have I been more moved than I was after meeting Linda.

What gave this woman the purpose and radiance she obviously experienced? What motivated her to strive for fulfillment and accomplishment? I knew that Linda would answer those questions without hesitation: Jesus Christ had given her real life.

Can Jesus really affect the way in which Linda and others live their daily lives? Should there be any noticeable difference between the person who believes in Christ and the one who doesn't?

The Bible indicates that knowing Christ is the most exciting adventure the human mind can comprehend. This adventure is waiting for those who love our Lord. Open your heart and your life to this adventure. You'll never be sorry.

HIS WORD
"The fruit of the Spirit is love, joy, peace, patience, kindness, goodness, faithfulness, gentleness and self-control. Against such things there is no law" *(Galatians 5:22,23).*

MY PART
The Christian lifestyle is not one of legalistic do's and don'ts, but one that is positive, attractive, and joyful. How do you represent Christianity? Be different from the world. Yield to Christ to let His love shine through you no matter what your circumstances may be.

MY STUDY
Deuteronomy 26:16; Psalm 15:1–5

DAY 78

Jay sat on the floor of a bookstore with his four-year-old daughter, Samantha. She snuggled in his lap while he read her a Sesame Street book. Jay loved to read to Samantha. When she saw a word she recognized, she was quick to help him read the story.

Tender Hearts

Teachable moments come spontaneously with children, and Jay always tried to capture those moments to impart a biblical truth.

Jay's animated reading style attracted the attention of a nearby six-year-old who couldn't resist plopping down in front of Jay and Samantha to listen in.

As Jay moved his head back and forth to imitate the Sesame Street character, he asked Samantha, "Who made Big Bird?"

"God," his daughter confidently answered.

"Who?" their new six-year-old friend asked. She was genuinely puzzled. It was as though she'd never heard such a question before. Samantha did a great "four-year-old" explanation of God's work in creation. The wide-eyed listener seemed a bit dismayed that a four-year-old knew something she didn't. As Jay watched the girls interacting, he realized how precious those teachable moments were. At home that evening, Jay talked to his wife about having a structured time when the neighborhood children could come to their home for storytime.

It was a great idea, and from that day in the bookstore, they've used a weekly storytime to share Christian love with the neighborhood children. It has proved to be a great time to insert biblical concepts that have opened many questions by the children as well as their parents.

Make sure your heart is tender toward children. Take time for them and teach them about God's love. This is the most priceless gift you can give them.

HIS WORD
"Come, my children, listen to me; I will teach you the fear of the Lord" (Psalm 34:11).

MY PART
If you have the opportunity to be with young children, please do not assume that concepts about God and His character are too deep for their understanding. Children can embrace concepts about God that lay a foundation for all their future understanding. Share biblical truths as God gives you opportunity.

MY STUDY
Deuteronomy 4:9,10; Ephesians 6:4

The story of Jill and Rob is one that is played out many times. It is difficult to identify when or where the problem started, but for this Christian couple the reality came when they moved from a small town to a big city. Perhaps the stress of moving magnified their problems, but suddenly their marriage was in crisis. Jill felt lonely. Rob felt unfulfilled. By any counselor's standards, the red flags were flying.

Warning Signs

Life in a new city was defined by loneliness and isolation for Jill. The one person who could provide comfort was the very one she withdrew from. Jill loved Rob, but any attempt to express her love failed.

Jill was faithful in her Bible reading and had found God's Word to provide comfort and direction many times in the past. However, now when she read her Bible, there was something different. One cloudy morning as she sat curled up in her chair, she read the passage in 1 Peter 3. Wow, there it was!

What Jill hadn't realized was that a seed of resentment had begun to grow in her heart from the time they decided to move. She had allowed that seed to flourish and grow. Now it was keeping her from expressing love and support to her husband. Everyday, Jill sincerely prayed for her own life and for her husband's. Soon a freedom came for her to express her love to Rob.

At first Rob didn't pick up on the change in Jill's attitude. But within six months, Jill noticed a marked difference in their relationship. He began to initiate expressions of love for Jill and finally restored the joy of his salvation.

Rob and Jill now share a fresh excitement about their faith, and Jill has the joy of hearing Rob publicly acknowledge the part she played in helping them rediscover their love for each other and their love for Jesus Christ.

HIS WORD

"However, each one of you also must love his wife as he loves himself, and the wife must respect her husband" (Ephesians 5:33).

MY PART

Remember, friends, actions speak louder than words. Jill applied the truth of God's Word to her heart and demonstrated her love to her husband. Do you have "warning signs" of impending trouble in your marriage? God will help you, but first you must acknowledge your need. Please do that today.

MY STUDY

Psalm 31:21–24; Jeremiah 32:40,41

riendships are forged in the good times and the bad.

That's what Catherine learned when her friend, Edwina, was diagnosed with breast cancer.

Friends Through the Fire

Before the discovery, these two women were casual friends. It was the crisis, however, that brought them close together.

After the doctor delivered the bad news, Catherine decided to check on Edwina every day, just to see how she was doing. Sometimes they'd talk for a few minutes; other times, for half an hour. Sometimes they'd laugh. Sometimes they'd cry. A true friendship was born.

Catherine was there when Edwina needed help caring for her children. Often, when returning from the doctor, they'd sit and talk. And cry. They went through lots of boxes of tissues during those months of treatment.

Catherine became a make-do hairdresser, trimming Edwina's hair when chemotherapy took its toll. She was an encourager, helping Edwina plan for the future. And she was a comic, making Edwina laugh when the weight of circumstances became too great. More than anything, Catherine just listened when Edwina needed to talk.

What a wonderful example of friendship. I think it's the kind of friendship mentioned in Proverbs 18:24: "There is a friend who sticks closer than a brother." In the good times and the bad.

You may know someone who's going through a difficult time right now. Would you be that Proverbs kind of friend to that person? Can you reach out like Catherine did? I'm afraid sometimes our good intentions fail for lack of action. We think great thoughts but don't follow through with them. We intend to provide comfort but get too busy. We hear about a friend's trial but fail to pray with her.

Put your faith into action today.

HIS WORD

"Therefore encourage one another and build each other up, just as in fact you are doing" (1 Thessalonians 5:11).

MY PART

Don't allow feelings of inadequacy to stop you. Edwina didn't need people to say anything. She needed someone to listen and to care. Perhaps you know someone who has just lost a mate or a child. Or maybe a friend of yours is going through a divorce. Ask God to show you how to reach out to those who are hurting.

MY STUDY

1 Samuel 23:16–18; Psalm 37:3

After fifty-two years of marriage, I have a greater appreciation for my dear husband than ever before. He's a wonderful person—loving, kind, wise, faithful. I respect and trust him completely.

It's the Little Things

Yet, like everyone else I know, we have occasional conflicts. Those moments are usually inspired by a petty, little issue. We have one story we've told so many times that our Crusade staff call it the "Knife Story."

The kitchen is usually my domain, but Bill had been complaining about the dullness of our kitchen knives. One night to my dismay, Bill came home with a large, very expensive set of new knives. He thought I'd be happy! He bragged about their virtues: they'd never need sharpening and could cut through anything, including steel.

I strongly objected. They were black in an ugly brown box, and I could just imagine how awful they'd look on my pretty white counter.

My solution was to buy a knife sharpener for our old

expensive knives. After we each defended our purchases, things grew very quiet between us.

Finally, we realized what was happening. We were harboring resentment toward each other over a very minor thing.

Too many misunderstandings start with ridiculous things like this. There's only one solution: have enough courage to say, "I'm so sorry. I was wrong. Please forgive me. I love you." You must be willing to resolve the little conflicts.

Bill and I are careful to keep Christ in control of our lives. We pray together when we wake up and just before we fall asleep. Nothing has brought more harmony in our marriage than prayer.

You'll never guess what happened to those knives. In the end, I gave them to Bill as a gift. And he gave me the knife sharpener! Both are great reminders that we value each other much more than conflict and cutlery combined!

HIS WORD
"Wives, in the same way be submissive to your husbands…"
(1 Peter 3:1).

MY PART
If you're married, let me encourage you to make a commitment to pursue peace every day. And pray together. When our eyes are focused on God, the little irritations resume their perspective—insignificant.

MY STUDY
Genesis 2:24;
Psalm 25:9

The five Warner brothers amassed a fortune through their family business. They've made some of the most successful films in the history of Hollywood. When the last surviving brother cashed out of his Warner Brothers stock, it was worth $640 million.

True Friends

A curious reporter posed this question of Jack Warner: "Jack, after all you've accomplished in the business, you must have a lot of friends. How many friends do you have?"

Jack Warner, one of the wealthiest men in America at that time, gave the reporter this sad response, "I don't have one."

Not a single friend! How tragic to have achieved such financial success, yet have no one to call your friend. Think about what you're doing to develop good friendships. Are you pursuing friendships with others and making real efforts to *be* a good friend?

Let me offer some thoughts for you to consider.

Being a good friend takes time. Both scheduled and spontaneous times are essential to friendship.

A good friend is forgiving. When mistakes are made,

the words, "I'm sorry," need to come easily. I've heard it said this way: "True friends don't rub it in ...but they choose to rub it out."

A good friend can keep a secret. Friends must have absolute confidence that their discussions never leave the room. Nothing will drive a wedge any quicker than betrayal of this trust.

A true friend is honest. Don't allow yourself to gloss over problem areas. If you spot a flaw, first pray about it and seek God's direction about saying something. In Proverbs 27:5,6 we read, "Better is open rebuke than hidden love. Wounds from a friend can be trusted."

Finally...*Good friends never quit.* When life becomes intense, a true friend hangs in there. Hold onto them even tighter than you would your greatest earthly treasure.

True friends are precious gifts from God. Hold them close to your heart.

HIS WORD
"A man of many companions may come to ruin, but there is a friend who sticks closer than a brother" (Proverbs 18:24).

MY PART
Author and scholar C. S. Lewis said, "Is there any pleasure on earth as great as a circle of Christian friends by a fire?" Treasure your friends. Let them know how you feel. And pray for them daily.

MY STUDY
Daniel 12:3; Philippians 2:19–23

Read the words of Jesus from John 15:15: "I no longer call you servants, because a servant does not know his master's business. Instead, I have called you friends, for everything that I learned from my Father I have made known to you."

A Life of Sharing

As Christians, our mission is to share the friendship we have with Jesus with those who don't know Him personally, and then help them grow in their new faith.

I began at an early age to see how rewarding a life of sharing can be. When I was growing up, Mother and Dad loved to invite friends to our home. Some of my earliest recollections are of Mother teaching me to pass out napkins, to wait to be served last, and to pay attention to details that make guests feel comfortable and appreciated.

In those days, the population of Coweta, Oklahoma, was only 1,500, but we enjoyed an amazing number of formal events. Several professional couples had moved to the community, and it was important to them to preserve some of the culture they brought with them.

As a child, I observed afternoon teas and candlelight dinners. As a teenager, I enjoyed formal parties and looked forward to the ice cream socials and watermelon feeds held by churches and various groups in the summer. I was so impressed with these events that I thought, *It'll be so much fun to go to these parties when I'm grown up.*

Home and hospitality were so important to me that I chose to major in home economics in college. I didn't know at the time how God would use the things I was learning.

Of course, God knew all about me and about the plans He had for my life. None of my desires were a surprise to Him!

After many years of ministry, I'm even more excited about how sharing our lives through hospitality can influence people. It is a tool to help open their hearts.

HIS WORD

"Offer hospitality to one another without grumbling. Each one should use whatever gift he has received to serve others, faithfully administering God's grace in its various forms" *(1 Peter 4:9,10).*

MY PART

As Christians, we have the privilege of extending hospitality to those who may not even recognize their need for God. Our gesture of hospitality may be as simple as coffee and cookies at home or sharing a muffin with a co-worker. Look for these opportunities, then graciously do them.

MY STUDY

2 Kings 4:8–17; Proverbs 11:25

You would never have guessed that Brenda was a battered wife. She lived in a beautiful neighborhood, and her family was in church every Sunday. But as she gradually withdrew, no one in the church noticed.

No one, that is, except Eva.

Always Learning

Eva, an older woman, was concerned. She didn't believe it when Brenda's husband said that she had emotional problems. Eva's suspicions grew when he insisted that no one should visit her.

Eva and Brenda gradually developed a relationship. Finally, Brenda admitted the truth. She'd been too embarrassed to tell her other friends, but Eva's love and compassion broke through.

Eva became a spiritual mentor to Brenda. Over time, restoration and healing were brought into that troubled home.

A Bible story about two women gives us a further example of how a friendship can provide strength. Mary was unmarried and pregnant. She was filled with emotions—excited to be expecting, but embarrassed about her status. When she traveled to see her cousin, she was not sure what the reaction would be to her circumstances.

Her cousin was delighted to see her and invited her to stay for an extended visit. They were together for the next three months, sharing a critical time in any woman's life —the expectancy of a first child.

I'm speaking, of course, about Mary, the mother of Jesus, and Elizabeth, the mother of John the Baptist. God used Elizabeth to confirm His promise to Mary and affirm Mary's faith and character.

Every woman can benefit from the wisdom of another woman. Prayerfully consider the women you know and identify someone you respect and admire. Cultivate a relationship that would allow you to feel confident in seeking advice or sharing your struggles. God can use another woman to provide help and hope at any age.

HIS WORD

"My soul will boast in the Lord; let the afflicted hear and rejoice. Glorify the Lord with me; let us exalt his name together" (Psalm 34:2,3).

MY PART

"Heavenly Father, thank You for giving us friendships that allow us to love and support each other. Help me to seek mentors and to be a mentor to others so we may grow in Your love and grace. In Jesus' holy name, amen."

MY STUDY

Ruth 3:1–5;
Acts 11:25,26

Frances Green was eighty-three years old and lived alone in San Francisco. She had very little, but gave one dollar a year to support the Republican National Committee.

Try a Little Kindness

One day, she received an elegant invitation to come to the White House to meet President Reagan. Friends helped her save enough to make the trip. What Frances didn't notice, however, was the RSVP note inside her envelope, the one that required a substantial contribution in order to be included.

When she arrived at the White House gate, this dear elderly lady was turned away by the guard. Her name didn't appear on his official list. She was devastated.

Behind her in line was a kind man who overheard her conversation with the guard. He could tell what had happened, so he asked her to meet him at nine o'clock the next morning at the White House. She agreed.

When Frances arrived the following morning, this gentleman had arranged for a wonderful White House tour. He personally guided her and talked about the many wonderful rooms and historical items.

When Frances and her escort arrived at the Oval Office, high-ranking generals were coming and going. Then President Reagan spotted Frances outside the door.

He got up from his desk and said, "Ah, Frances! Those computers, they fouled up again! If I'd known you were coming, I would have come out there to get you myself!"

He invited Frances to join him in the Oval Office. There they chatted about California, her family, and how she was doing.

The President knew this woman had nothing to give. But he knew he had something to give Frances. He gave her compassion and kindness.

A little kindness can make the difference in someone's life. And it is so easy to share!

HIS WORD

"Therefore, as God's chosen people, holy and dearly loved, clothe yourselves with compassion, kindness, humility, gentleness and patience" (Colossians 3:12).

MY PART

In our high-tech and demanding culture, we're often rushing to and from events, never taking time to stop and consider those around us who have profound needs. Let's learn a lesson from one of our nation's great patriots. Take time to share the love of Jesus with those who are waiting at the gate, perhaps without a ticket to enter in.

MY STUDY

Genesis 50:15–21; Jeremiah 9:24

When I first began to read and study the Bible, I considered it great literature. And it is. I found it a fascinating historical record, but the Bible is so much more. By studying God's Holy Word, I've come to appreciate it for the wonderful ways it speaks to every dimension of life.

A Gentle Answer

In each aspect of my life—every decision, every relationship, every problem—the Bible has something to say. It instructs me on what to do and how to have healthy attitudes. That's why I read the Bible every day. I consult it constantly. When I do, I understand God's way. So does my friend Sallie.

Recently, Sallie moved into a new home. Several large limbs from a neighbor's tree hung over Sallie's back fence. They needed to be trimmed.

Sallie consulted a tree surgeon. She approached her neighbors to explain the situation. The woman of the household gave Sallie a verbal agreement to do whatever was necessary.

The workmen came and began to cut the limbs. The neighbor's husband was the only one home that day, and apparently his wife hadn't told him about the tree-trimming.

He was furious. The workers referred him, of course, to Sallie.

Can you imagine Sallie's surprise when her irate neighbor appeared at her front door?

In the midst of this frightening encounter, God brought to her mind His Word. God reminded her of Proverbs 15:1. It says, "A gentle answer turns away wrath, but a harsh word stirs up anger."

She said, "Oh, I am *so* sorry. There must be some misunderstanding...I need a neighbor a lot worse than I need the tree work done."

The answer helped to calm the situation, and together they found a solution. The neighbor apologized and a relationship began to develop that day. Truly, a gentle answer can work miracles!

HIS WORD
"Let your gentleness be evident to all. The Lord is near" (Philippians 4:5).

MY PART
As you grow in your understanding of how to apply God's Word, your life will be changed. Read your Bible daily, asking God for wisdom to apply it to your life. Then you will begin to observe some exciting changes in your life and heart.

MY STUDY
Proverbs 14:29; Isaiah 40:11

There's nothing like a mature, wise friend to give us counsel and direction. As a seasoned veteran with a depth of experience, a mature friend can share wisdom unavailable elsewhere.

A Helping Hand

I heard about a church in Southern California where older couples attend the Sunday school classes of younger people. These couples don't teach the class; they simply attend all the events and become acquainted with everyone who comes. By their presence, they provide an example, a model to follow. The more mature adults often counsel their younger friends, or pray for them, as the need arises.

Sometimes it's a joyful experience—celebrating a promotion or the birth of a baby. Other times, mentoring younger couples requires tremendous strength and sensitivity—helping husbands and wives resolve conflict, showing how to handle problems with in-laws, or dealing with tragedy in their lives.

What a wonderful way to strengthen the body of Christ!

So many young people enter marriage without a model. Often, their parents are divorced. It's so helpful to have someone at church who's advising them, taking them under their wing, praying for them —mentoring them.

It doesn't require a special program, or have to fit the context of a Sunday school class. You might reach out to someone in your neighborhood. Regardless of your age, you have talents and gifts to contribute to the family of God— especially to someone younger.

To mentor others, we must be real with them, sharing our joys and sorrows. We must give of our time and our wealth of experience.

Of this I am absolutely sure: as you minister to others, your life will be enriched! For as you serve one another, you are a reflection of God's love.

HIS WORD
"I thought, 'Age should speak; advanced years should teach wisdom.' But it is the spirit in a man, the breath of the Almighty, that gives him understanding. It is not only the old who are wise, not only the aged who understand what is right" (Job 32:7–9).

MY PART
Look for ways to reach out to younger and older women who need you. Establish relationships. Let them know you're praying for them. Invite them to visit in your home. Talk openly about your relationship with God, and find ways to encourage and support them.

MY STUDY
Proverbs 31:20; Romans 16:1,2

James Bryan Smith tells this story in his wonderful book, *Embracing the Love of God*.

At first, the call was a bit mysterious. Though the voice sounded familiar, it had been a long time since James had heard it.

Loving Your Neighbor

It was Marge, a neighbor from years earlier. Marge still lived in the home behind the house where James grew up, but *his* family had long since moved.

Marge asked about his mother. "I was trying to reach your mother. Where does she live now?"

James gave her his mother's telephone number. Then Marge explained why she was asking. Her oldest son had recently died of complications related to the AIDS virus. "I just need to talk to your mom," Marge said. "She's always so accepting. No matter what happens, I know I can always call her and she will stand by me. I love your mom so much."

How we all need someone in our lives like James's

mother. And we all need to *be* that kind of neighbor in the lives of others.

James's mother was a neighbor others could call on. She had a listening ear and a compassionate heart. Even when separated by distance and time, a neighbor in need remembered her gentle manner.

In 2 Corinthians 1:4, the apostle Paul writes, "[God] comforts us in all our trouble, so that we can comfort those in any trouble with the comfort we ourselves have received from God."

Have you cultivated the kind of attitude that allows others to feel they can confide in you in their times of need? Do you emanate a spirit of acceptance or of criticism? Comfort others as God has comforted you, then give Him all the glory.

HIS WORD
"The second [greatest commandment] is this: 'Love your neighbor as yourself'" (Mark 12:31).

MY PART
Are you the neighbor someone could come to for compassion, understanding, and comfort? Today, open your door—the door to your home and the door to your heart. Reach out with God's love. Embrace and comfort your neighbors with your attention, concern, and His Words of truth.

MY STUDY
Leviticus 19:18; Proverbs 22:2

Donna and Kimberly met at a church committee meeting. They immediately liked each other. Kim was young, single, and just getting started. Donna was married and well-established. At the end of their conversation, Kim told Donna to call her if there was any way she could help her.

A Daughter of the Heart

Donna Otto tells this story in her book *Between Women of God*.

A few weeks after meeting Kim, Donna got really busy with a big project. She was so involved, she didn't have time to run needed errands. Then she remembered Kim and her offer to help. So she called her.

Donna asked Kim if she could run those errands. Kim hesitated, then explained, "I'd love to, but I don't have a car."

Donna offered her the use of a car. Kim explained she actually had a car, but couldn't afford the insurance. She said, "I'm disciplining myself to ride the bus as a way to get my finances in order."

Donna and her husband, David, had been discussing

what to do with their home. With their daughter away at college, it seemed too large and empty. They'd prayed for someone they could take into their home. Kim might be the answer to those prayers.

"Well," Donna said, "if you came to live with us for thirty days, you would have the money for the car insurance *and* you could help me a few hours a week in return."

Kim not only moved into Donna and David's home, she moved into their hearts. She didn't stay for just a month, she stayed for two years. Donna says Kim became a "daughter of her heart."

They worked together, prayed together, laughed together, and had a few spats together. By the time she moved into her own apartment, she was debt-free and had a savings account.

That, my friend, is a wonderful picture of the art of mentoring.

HIS WORD
"If anyone has material possessions and sees his brother in need but has no pity on him, how can the love of God be in him? Dear children, let us not love with words or tongue but with actions and in truth" (1 John 3;17,18).

MY PART
"Heavenly Father, open my eyes to see creative ways to reach out to someone. I want to invest my life in others. You have been so generous with me and I am so thankful for Your guidance. Please make me a blessing! Amen."

MY STUDY
Isaiah 32:8; Psalm 41:1–3

All relationships have a measure of misunderstanding, hurt, and pain. And in this fallen world, there's certainly no such thing as a perfect marriage. Disagreeing on occasion doesn't mean you don't love each other.

Words To Save a Marriage

Bill and I have been married fifty-two years. Because longevity in a relationship has become quite rare in this culture, I'm often asked to identify our secret.

We've decided any marriage will survive if the partners will memorize and use just twelve words. You could probably guess what they are:

"I love you."

"I am sorry."

"I was wrong."

"Please forgive me."

Sometimes uttering those twelve simple words can be tough to do in the heat of emotional battle. But in a healthy marriage, practicing forgiveness must come easy.

A friend teases me about the time she heard me

talking to my husband on the phone. She says she knew we were having a disagreement because she first heard me call him "Honey," then "Bill," and then "Bill Bright."

As my terms intensified, so did the tone of my voice! When that happens, I pray, "Lord, give me the power to love Bill like you love him. Don't let me get stuck in these momentary feelings of frustration with him."

Then I'm able to swallow hard and speak those simple words.

I must admit the few times when my husband has hurt my feelings, I've been tempted to hurt him back. When he said something offensive, I wanted to respond in the same tone.

I know that's a silly and immature attitude. It doesn't accomplish anything.

But with God's help, we can be sensitive to our mate and love him as God expects us to.

HIS WORD

"If you are offering your gift at the altar and there remember that your brother has something against you, leave your gift there in front of the altar. First go and be reconciled to your brother; then come and offer your gift" *(Matthew 5:23,24).*

MY PART

When we determine that divorce is not an option, it's only by God's power that we can work through our differences and truly understand each other. In a loving way, we can communicate and resolve whatever conflict comes our way.

MY STUDY

Proverbs 3:3; Job 22:29

Beginning Your Journey of Joy

These four principles are essential in beginning a journey of joy.

One—God loves you and created you to know Him personally.

God's Love

"God so loved the world that He gave His one and only Son, that whoever believes in Him shall not perish but have eternal life" (John 3:16).

God's Plan

"Now this is eternal life: that they may know you, the only true God, and Jesus Christ, whom you have sent" (John 17:3).

What prevents us from knowing God personally?

Two—People are sinful and separated from God, so we cannot know Him personally or experience His love.

People are Sinful

"All have sinned and fall short of the glory of God" (Romans 3:23).

People were created to have fellowship with God; but, because of our own stubborn self-will, we chose to go our own independent way and fellowship with God was broken. This self-will, characterized by an attitude of active rebellion or passive indifference, is an evidence of what the Bible calls sin.

People are Separated

"The wages of sin is death" [spiritual separation from God] (Romans 6:23).

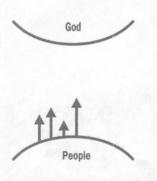

This diagram illustrates that God is holy and people are sinful. A great gulf separates the two. The arrows illustrate that people are continually trying to reach God and establish a personal relationship with Him through our own efforts, such as a good life, philosophy, or religion—but we inevitably fail.

The third principle explains the only way to bridge this gulf...

Three—Jesus Christ is God's only provision for our sin. Through Him alone we can know God personally and experience His love.

He Died In Our Place

"God demonstrates His own love toward us, in that while we were yet sinners, Christ died for us" (Romans 5:8).

He Rose from the Dead

"Christ died for our sins…He was buried…He was raised on the third day according to the Scriptures…He appeared to Peter, then to the twelve. After that He appeared to more than five hundred…" (1 Corinthians 15:3–6).

He Is the Only Way to God

"Jesus said to him, 'I am the way, and the truth, and the life; no one comes to the Father but through Me'" (John 14:6).

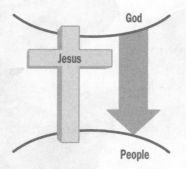

This diagram illustrates that God has bridged the gulf that separates us from Him by sending His Son, Jesus Christ, to die on the cross in our place to pay the penalty for our sins.

It is not enough just to know these three truths…

Four—We must individually receive Jesus Christ as Savior and Lord; then we can know God personally and experience His love.

We Must Receive Christ

"As many as received Him, to them He gave the right to become children of God, even to those who believe in His name" (John 1:12).

We Receive Christ Through Faith
"By grace you have been saved through faith; and that not of yourselves, it is the gift of God; not as a result of works that no one should boast" (Ephesians 2:8,9).

When We Receive Christ, We Experience a New Birth
(Read John 3:1–8.)

We Receive Christ By Personal Invitation
[Christ speaking] "Behold, I stand at the door and knock; if anyone hears My voice and opens the door, I will come in to him" (Revelation 3:20).

Receiving Christ involves turning to God from self (repentance) and trusting Christ to come into our lives to forgive us of our sins and to make us what He wants us to be. Just to agree intellectually that Jesus Christ is the Son of God and that He died on the cross for our sins is not enough. Nor is it enough to have an emotional experience. We receive Jesus Christ by faith, as an act of our will.

These two circles represent two kinds of lives:

Self-Directed Life
S – Self is on the throne
† – Christ is outside the life
● – Interests are directed by self, often resulting in discord and frustration

Christ-Directed Life
† – Christ is in the life and on the throne
S – Self is yielding to Christ
● – Interests are directed by Christ, resulting in harmony with God's plan

Which circle best represents your life?
Which circle would you like to have represent your life?

The following explains how you can receive Christ:

You Can Receive Christ Right Now by Faith Through Prayer

(Prayer is talking with God)

God knows your heart and is not so concerned with your words as He is with the attitude of your heart. The following is a suggested prayer:

> *Lord Jesus, I want to know You personally. Thank You for dying on the cross for my sins. I open the door of my life and receive You as my Savior and Lord. Thank You for forgiving my sins and giving me eternal life. Take control of the throne of my life. Make me the kind of person You want me to be.*

Does this prayer express the desire of your heart?

If it does, I invite you to pray this prayer right now, and Christ will come into your life, as He promised.

How to Know That Christ Is in Your Life

Did you receive Christ into your life? According to His promise in Revelation 3:20, where is Christ right now in relation to you? Christ said that He would come into your life. Would He mislead you? On what authority do you know that God has answered your prayer? (The trustworthiness of God Himself and His Word.)

The Bible Promises Eternal Life to All Who Receive Christ

"The witness is this, that God has given us eternal life, and this life is in His Son. He who has the Son has the life; he who does not have the Son of God does not have

the life. These things I have written to you who believe in the name of the Son of God, in order that you may know that you have eternal life" (1 John 5:11–13).

Thank God often that Christ is in your life and that He will never leave you (Hebrews 13:5). You can know on the basis of His promise that Christ lives in you and that you have eternal life from the very moment you invite Him in. He will not deceive you.

An important reminder…

Feelings Can Be Unreliable

You might have expectations about how you should feel after placing your trust in Christ. While feelings are important, they are unreliable indicators of your sincerity or the trustworthiness of God's promise. Our feelings change easily, but God's Word and His character remain constant. This illustration shows the relationship among **fact** (God and His Word), **faith** (our trust in God and His Word), and our **feelings**.

Fact: The chair is strong enough to support you.
Faith: You believe this chair will support you, so you sit in it.

Feeling: You may or may not feel comfortable in this chair, but it continues to support you.

The promise of God's Word, the Bible—not our feelings —is our authority. The Christian lives by faith (trust) in the trustworthiness of God Himself and His Word.

Now That You Have Entered Into a Personal Relationship With Christ

The moment you received Christ by faith, as an act of your will, many things happened, including the following:

- Christ came into your life (Revelation 3:20; Colossians 1:27).
- Your sins were forgiven (Colossians 1:14).
- You became a child of God (John 1:12).
- You received eternal life (John 5:24).
- You began the great adventure for which God created you (John 10:10; 2 Corinthians 5:17; 1 Thessalonians 5:18).

Can you think of anything more wonderful that could happen to you than entering into a personal relationship with Jesus Christ? Would you like to thank God in prayer right now for what He has done for you? By thanking God, you demonstrate your faith.

To enjoy your new relationship with God…

Suggestions for Christian Growth

Spiritual growth results from trusting Jesus Christ. "The righteous man shall live by faith" (Galatians 3:11). A life

of faith will enable you to trust God increasingly with every detail of your life, and to practice the following:

G Go to God in prayer daily (John 15:7).

R Read God's Word daily (Acts 17:11); begin with the Gospel of John.

O Obey God moment by moment (John 14:21).

W Witness for Christ by your life and words (Matthew 4:19; John 15:8).

T Trust God for every detail of your life (1 Peter 5:7).

H Holy Spirit—allow Him to control and empower your daily life and witness (Galatians 5:16,17; Acts 1:8; Ephesians 5:18).

Fellowship in a Good Church

God's Word admonishes us not to forsake "the assembling of ourselves together" (Hebrews 10:25). Several logs burn brightly together, but put one aside on the cold hearth and the fire goes out. So it is with your relationship with other Christians. If you do not belong to a church, do not wait to be invited. Take the initiative; call the pastor of a nearby church where Christ is honored and His Word is preached. Start this week, and make plans to attend regularly.

Resources

My Heart in His Hands: Renew a Steadfast Spirit Within Me. Spring—renewal is everywhere; we are reminded to cry out to God, "Renew a steadfast spirit within me." The first of four books in Vonette Bright's new devotional series, this book will give fresh spiritual vision and hope to women of all ages. ISBN 1-56399-161-6

My Heart in His Hands: I Delight Greatly in My Lord. Do you stop to appreciate the blessings God has given you? Spend time delighting in God with book three in this devotional series. ISBN 1-56399-163-2

My Heart in His Hands: Lead Me in the Way Everlasting. We all need guidance, and God is the ultimate leader. These daily moments with God will help you to rely on His leadership. The final in the four-book devotional series. ISBN 1-56399-164-0

The Joy of Hospitality: Fun Ideas for Evangelistic Entertaining. Co-written with Barbara Ball, this practical book tells how to share your faith through hosting barbecues, coffees, holiday parties, and other events in your home. ISBN 1-56399-057-1

The Joy of Hospitality Cookbook. Filled with uplifting scriptures and quotations, this cookbook contains hundreds of delicious recipes, hospitality tips, sample menus, and family traditions that are sure to make your entertaining a memorable and eternal success. Co-written with Barbara Ball. ISBN 1-56399-077-6

The Greatest Lesson I've Ever Learned. In this treasury of inspiring, real-life experiences, twenty-three prominent women of faith share their "greatest lessons." Does God have faith- and character-building lessons for you in their rich, heart-warming stories? ISBN 1-56399-085-7

Beginning Your Journey of Joy. This adaptation of the *Four Spiritual Laws* speaks in the language of today's women and offers a slightly feminine approach to sharing God's love with your neighbors, friends, and family members. ISBN 1-56399-093-8

These and other fine products from *NewLife* Publications are available from your favorite bookseller or by calling (800) 235-7255 (within U.S.) or (407) 826-2145, or by visiting www.newlifepubs.com.